The Spokesman

A Special Relationship ... with 1

Edited by Ken Coates
Assistant Editor Tony Simpson

Published by Spokesman for th
Bertrand Russell Peace Foundation

K)
; UK)

Spokesman 108   **2010**

CONTENTS

Editorial
Special Relationship? **3** *Ken Coates*

Lord Goldsmith and Iraq **9** *Sir Edmund Thomas QC*

Parade of the Old New **26** *Bertolt Brecht*

Another Agenda **27** *Bob Marshall-Andrews MP*

Demockracy **30** *Bob Dixon*

Britain Can't **32** *Scott Ritter*
Handle the Truth

Writing *Principia* **36** *Bertrand Russell*

Kurt Is up in Heaven Now **43** *Kurt Vonnegut*

Farewell Michael Foot **46**

Judgment **48** *Lord Judge*
Lord Neuberger

Spooks Sold **51** *Clive Stafford Smith*
down the River

The Chilcot Enquiry **53** *Alexis Lykiard*

Carnage in Gaza **54** *Nurit Peled Elhanan*

Dossier **59** *Russell Tribunal*
on Palestine

Reviews **65** *Christopher Gifford,*
Henry McCubbin,
Bill Hagerty, Tony Simpson,
Nathaniel Mehr,
Ken Coates, John Daniels,
J.E. Mortimer, Frank Barat,
Graham Hallett, Abi Rhodes

Cover *Steve Bell*

A CIP catalogue record
for this book is available
from the British Library

Published by the
Bertrand Russell Peace
Foundation Ltd.,
Russell House
Bulwell Lane
Nottingham NG6 0BT
England
Tel. 0115 9784504
email:
elfeuro@compuserve.com
www.spokesmanbooks.com
www.russfound.org

FSC
Mixed Sources
Product group from well-managed
forests and other controlled sources

Cert no. SGS-COC-006541
www.fsc.org
© 1996 Forest Stewardship Council

ISSN 1367 7748   Printed by the Russell Press Ltd., Nottingham, UK   ISBN 978 0 85124 777 9

Editorial
Special Relationship?

We recently gave our attention to the strange mutations which have taken place in the British constitution as a result of developments in the alleged intelligence services. As we observed, their trade in intelligence proper has not always been attended by much success, but regardless of this disadvantage their influence has grown and grown.

It would not be unfair to remark that this process has been accompanied by another, not dissimilar: the never-ending continuity of the so-called special relationship, between Britain and the United States. This, too, has hardly been immune from the processes of change. It began with a rather different shape from its present one, but from lusty young robber to decrepit old monster, it has developed, with ubiquity, a distinct modesty, which means that it is hardly ever discussed objectively in its own right. True, permitted are endless rather flatulent commentaries in which the deep ties of consanguinity and linguistic affinity are hymned. But what it is all for, and how its mechanisms are arranged, is not a matter to discuss in front of the children.

If one studied official American military doctrine, one could be excused for failing to find any relationships, anywhere, but those of subordination. 'Full Spectrum Dominance' is still the official credo of the American military-industrial complex, and there, it might be thought, is an end of it. But Britain is perhaps unique among the dominated in seeking actually to celebrate its subordination. That is why it was so refreshing to hear Clare Short testifying before the Chilcot Inquiry.

When Sir John asked her if she had any comments to make on the re-evaluation of her experiences, which she had described with some candour, she said that she thought that her old Department of International Development had not been adequately involved; that the machinery of Government 'has broken down quite badly'; and that the role of the Attorney General must be adjudged unsafe following his various pronouncements on the legality of the war. But then she added a fourth comment, braver than all the others, which broke new ground for the Inquiry. The fourth problem, she said,

> 'is about the special relationship. We really need a serious debate in our country about what we mean by it, whether it is unconditional poodle-like adoration and do whatever America says, or whether we have bottom lines and we sometimes agree and we sometimes don't and we use our influence

responsibly, and I think we have ended up humiliating ourselves and being a less good friend to America than we could have been if we had stood up for an independent policy.

But that's a bigger question, because you should see, when America asks for something, the Prime Minister and the Chancellor all get terribly excited and love America asking us to do something, and we really need to rethink that.

Those are my lessons.'

We have been seeing more than is usually visible of the special relationship of late. Firstly, Britain is about to enter a diplomatic shunt, if not something worse, on the vexed old question of the Falkland Islands. It is thought that much oil is about to be extracted, and the Argentinians are not unnaturally anxious, as once were the Scots, to have their share. Thirty-odd South and Central American countries have given their approval to this desire. Ever anchored in the special relationship, President Obama sits on the special fence which prevents him from untoward solidarity with his special ally. On this occasion, many of us will not disapprove of the President's choice. But all of us, whatever we think of the rights and wrongs of ancient British imperial acquisitions in the South Atlantic, have had occasion to see the other face of the special relationship, presented in David Miliband's application to the Lord Chief Justice of England and Wales, the Master of the Rolls and the President of the Queen's Bench Division to overturn a judgment in the case of Binyam Mohamed.

The Court of Appeal ordered that seven paragraphs written by an officer of the British Security Services on the basis of reports from the United States intelligence agencies, which the Foreign Secretary had sought to suppress, should now be published. These read as follows:

'It was reported that a new series of interviews was conducted by the United States authorities prior to 17th May 2002 as part of a new strategy designed by an expert interviewer.

It was reported that at some stage during that further interview process by the United States authorities, Binyam Mohamed had been intentionally subjected to continuous sleep deprivation. The effects of the sleep deprivation were carefully observed.

It was reported that combined with the sleep deprivation, threats and inducements were made to him. His fears of being removed from United States custody and "disappearing" were played upon.

It was reported that the stress brought about by these deliberate tactics was increased by him being shackled in his interviews.

It was clear not only from the reports of the content of the interviews but also from the report that he was being kept under self-harm observation, that the interviews were having a marked effect upon him and causing him significant mental stress and suffering.

We regret to have to conclude that the reports provided to the Security Services [SyS] made clear to anyone reading them that Binyam Mohamed was being subjected to the treatment that we have described and the effect upon him of that intentional treatment.

The treatment reported, if it had been administered on behalf of the United Kingdom, would clearly have been in breach of the undertakings given by the United Kingdom in 1972. Although it is not necessary for us to categorise the treatment reported, it could readily be contended to be at the very least cruel, inhuman and degrading treatment by the United States authorities.'

The gist of these paragraphs had already been substantially published in the United States itself.

Previously we have reported the torture of Binyam Mohamed, and it is no longer disputed that he underwent a terrible ordeal. He was first held in Pakistan, thence rendered for eighteen months to Morocco, where his genitals were cut by scalpels whenever his interrogators took the whim. He was then taken to Afghanistan to the 'dark prison' in Kabul, where he was kept in total darkness, and endured other tortures for six months until he was transferred to Bagram, from where he was finally sent to Guantanamo for four years. All this, it might be thought, was a more than adequate experience of the special relationship.

From July 2008, Binyam's appeals to the Courts brought judgments that the British authorities were involved in wrongdoing, and that the Foreign Secretary needed to disclose forty-two secret documents received from the Americans to Binyam's lawyers. At this point, David Miliband claimed Public Interest Immunity. Publication would 'undermine the war on terror'. There followed an extensive exchange, selections from which we publish below.

At last Lord Neuberger and his colleagues have unanimously agreed on publication of the criticisms of the British Security Services. Promptly three most senior British Ministers followed one another to denounce this judgment. Alan Johnson, the Home Secretary, said he was 'deeply disappointed' by the negative remarks made about the Security Services. 'We totally reject any suggestion that the Security Services have a systemic problem in respecting human rights,' he said. 'We wholly reject, too, that they have any interest in suppressing or withholding information from Ministers or the Courts.' Mr. Miliband, hot from seeking the suppression of precisely the information in question, added his voice in the same vein. We also heard from the Prime Minister, robustly defending his intelligence men, heroes all. All feared jeopardy for the special relationship, in that, through promiscuous telling of the truth, the American willingness to exchange intelligence might be impaired.

Some of us think that this impairment might be very helpful, both in

---

Special intelligence relationship

In paragraph 93 of its judgment dated 10th February 2010, the Court of Appeal cited the views of an experienced former US official, Morton Halperin, on the intelligence relationship between the United Kingdom and the United States.

The court received a declaration dated 7th March 2009 from Morton Halperin, who had served three previous US Presidents (Johnson, Nixon and Clinton) challenging the notion that the US Government would review its communication of intelligence to the UK Government if the redacted paragraphs were released into the public domain. In his declaration, Mr Halperin explained that he had been 'exposed to the intelligence relationship between the [US] and the [UK] at the highest levels', most recently between 1998 and 2001, as director of Policy Planning Staff at the Department of State. He described the intelligence relationship between the two countries as 'unprecedented in its interdependence and depth' and 'staked on mutual trust and commitment to open dialogue and communication' for more than 60 years. He emphasised the benefits to the US, as well as the UK, of this relationship. He pointed out that both governments 'have always understood that the commitment to keep secret what was provided by the other could not be an absolute commitment', and referred to requests made under the Freedom of Information legislation, the fact that both governments understand that 'some information may reach the press and the public by leaks' and the fact that they 'also understand that courts in both countries have the right to order the disclosure of information under constitutional or statutory procedures'. He said that 'while the US government would expect the UK government to resist disclosure of classified information in this proceeding', 'a respect for the rule of law would prevent the US government from taking umbrage at a reasoned decision by a UK court finding that public interest demands disclosure of information regarding [Mr Mohamed]'. He also referred to cases where US courts had ordered disclosure of 'classified information obtained from foreign sources'.

Britain and America. Intelligence which 'beyond doubt' pinpointed the (non-existent) abundance of weapons of mass destruction in Iraq might better not have been shared, we heretically think. How much torture went into the preparation of the various British allegations, and how far were our American cousins involved in applying the necessary water boards? The sum total of human happiness might have been notably improved by the cessation of such intelligence gathering, and the obviation of any need to share its results. Creative interpretation of those results ('the intelligence and facts were being fixed around the policy') would also be eliminated by this beneficial change, were it ever to happen.

But disgusting though these depredations have all been, that is not the only disadvantage of the special relationship. It remains a symptom, not a cause. What has been happening is that over a long period of evolution, as the American military potency has increased, so the subordination of the allies has been augmented. Now the Britons are called upon, not for superior strategic counsel and manly example, but for a wide range of mercenary functions. We are still allowed to supply fodder for the imperial cannons. The cardinal virtue of subordinates in this relationship is now obedience, and the qualifications required by their statesmen are found predominantly in a dozen schools of sycophancy.

So Clare Short is right. It is time to talk about the special relationship. As Britain enters a General Election, this may indeed give rise to a deafening silence.

*   *   *

The Washington Post (Friday March 19th 2010) reports some unease about efforts to persuade senior officials of the Bush administration to brief the Chilcot Inquiry about their perspective on the war.

> 'We're hearing that the response from Bush administration folks has been decidedly cool, even though the panel apparently is willing to do the interviews in private, specify the subject areas in advance and accept statements on background, without naming names.'

The *Post* continues by saying that it has been the general view that

> 'while everyone was free to talk, "it was not right for American officials to be subject to a foreign investigative body". Former national security adviser Hadley, for example, was said to have been among those voicing a strong disinclination to participate.'

Wryly, the comment of *The Washington Post* is that there is 'still plenty of time to sign up!'

Evidently the Chilcot Inquiry fears that the hearing of foreign witnesses could be embarrassing. Sir John has declined to invite Dr. Amir Al Saadi to submit oral evidence, although he would accept written evidence if Dr. Al Saadi wished to submit it. Dr. Al Saadi was responsible for the preparation of the 12,000 page declaration submitted by the Iraqi Government in response to Resolution 1441 of the Security Council of the United Nations.

Although the Iraqi evidence was summarily dismissed by senior spokesmen of the Anglo-American alliance, including Jack Straw, subsequent events have revealed it to have been very much closer to the truth than the official view entertained by the British and American Governments. The special relationship is clearly well designed to get us into difficulties with the truth, but not the least of its advantages is that it can be suspended when necessary to avoid the subsequent problems which then arise.

Ken Coates

COMMUNICATION WORKERS UNION

May Day Greetings

NATO troops out of Afghanistan

Billy Hayes
General Secretary

Jane Loftus
President

Lord Goldsmith and Iraq

The Rt. Hon.
Sir Edmund Thomas
LLB (NZ) LLD (VUW) KNZM QC

The author is a retired Judge of the Court of Appeal of New Zealand and a former Acting Judge of the Supreme Court of New Zealand. In Spokesman 95, entitled War Crimes, *we published his groundbreaking article 'An indictment of Tony Blair, and the failure of the political process'. We are now pleased to publish, for the first time, his submission to the Iraq Inquiry about the role of the Attorney General, Lord Goldsmith, leading up to the war in Iraq.*

Introduction

I welcome the inquiry into the events leading up to and relating to the war in Iraq with the objective of identifying lessons that can be learned from those events. I respectfully proffer the following submission. It is restricted to the role of the Attorney General, Lord Goldsmith, in the lead-up to the war.

I was a senor partner in New Zealand's largest law firm for 32 years and a Queen's Counsel at the independent bar for 11 years. I became a Judge of the High Court in 1990. I was appointed to the Court of Appeal of New Zealand in 1995. I retired from that Court at the mandatory retirement age of 68 in 2001. After my retirement, the Government established the Supreme Court of New Zealand and I was recalled to serve as an Acting Supreme Court Judge. I retired from that position in 2008.

For the past five years I have been a Distinguished Visiting Fellow at the Law School at the University of Auckland. I have written a manuscript entitled, 'A Return to Principle in Judicial Reasoning and an Application of Judicial Autonomy' (1993) 23 *Victoria University of Wellington Law Review* Monograph 5, and a book entitled, *The Judicial Process: Realism, Pragmatism, Practical Reasoning and Principles* (Cambridge University Press, 2005). I have published over 50 articles relating to a wide range of legal topics. I have recently been awarded the higher degree of Doctorate of Laws (LLD) from Victoria University of Wellington.

In late 2006 I was invited to give a public lecture on a topic relating to international law. Although I initially intended to write about the Bush Administration's role in the lead-up to the war, I eventually directed my attention to the part played by the Prime Minister of Great Britain, Mr. Blair. The address was eventually published in *The Spokesman,* (2007) Vol. 95, p 12, under the title, 'An Indictment of Tony Blair, and the failure of the political process.'

As stated in the article, I sought to adhere to a judicial approach and judicial discipline in examining the various respects in which Mr. Blair might be held to have demonstrated a lack of probity in advancing the case for the invasion of Iraq. To this end, I read all the relevant books and available material. The authors' footnotes were carefully checked. I consider that my research was as thorough as it could be, short of a full inquiry of the kind the Committee is undertaking. In carrying out this research, my predisposition was to believe that Mr. Blair had been deluded, but sincere in his belief. The evidence convinced me otherwise and I was forced to conclude that Mr. Blair had repeatedly misled Cabinet, Parliament and the public in a number of respects. This conclusion led me to question how the Prime Minister's conduct could occur in a parliamentary democracy. I found that the political process had failed to constrain his actions. The shortcomings of that process quickly became the main focus of my article. (See *Spokesman 95* under the heading 'The failure of the political process', at p 42).

I appreciate that the Committee does not propose to pursue an inquiry into any possible criminal liability. To that extent it might be thought by some that the Inquiry is not intended to be a 'judicial' inquiry. Any such fine distinction, however, does not mean that the Committee will not wish to observe the characteristics that are loosely described as 'judicial', that is, exploring and undertaking a thorough examination of all relevant evidence, basing conclusions and recommendations on the evidence and observing the principles of natural justice. Hence, the Committee's approach may not be too different from the approach I sought to follow in my article.

One major difference, of course, is that the Committee will have access to vastly more evidence than is presently publicly available. The ability to demand access to critical documents and to summon and question key persons will prove invaluable. It is to be hoped that the Committee's final report will be the last word on what has been a divisive and controversial issue. To achieve that objective it will need to address a number of contentious issues that are of deep concern to many able and good people. The role of the Attorney General in the lead-up to the invasion is one of these concerns.

I wish to make an observation about the Committee's stated approach. While I agree that the task of identifying the lessons that can be learned from the conflict is of paramount importance and that it is not appropriate for the committee to make findings of guilt or innocence, I suspect that it may not be possible to avoid findings of fact that could constitute a criminal charge. I respectfully submit that this possibility is to be accepted without fear or favour. The consequences of the war have been far too traumatic for the nation, particularly the soldiers who have lost their lives and their families who now grieve and struggle with their loss, for it to be otherwise. In my own study, I would have found it difficult to identify the shortcomings in the political process and indicate reforms without first analysing the conduct of those responsible for leading the United Kingdom into the war. Similarly, I tend to think that the Committee may be impeded in arriving at the valuable lessons that can be learned from the events leading up to the conflict without first determining who was responsible for the various critical decisions that preceded the invasion. The one follows the other.

As already indicated, however, in this submission I wish to focus solely on the Attorney General's advice to the Prime Minister on the legality of the war. In an earlier article relating to the independence of the office of Attorney General in New Zealand (July (2009) *New Zealand Law Journal* 213), I repeated much of what I said in 2007 in relation to Lord Goldsmith's part in the lead up to the war. (See *Spokesman 95* at pp 27 to 33.)

I have selected this particular aspect because I suspect it is one which the Committee may find difficult. Unless they are of a different ilk from their counterparts in this country, the judiciary and the senior members of the legal profession will not be quick to criticise the Attorney General. Yet, the office of Attorney General is of fundamental constitutional importance and Lord Goldsmith's exercise of the powers of that office in the lead up to the war was undoubtedly of pivotal assistance in obtaining political and public support for the invasion.

I recognise that it may appear presumptuous for me to suggest lines of inquiry to the Committee. The added disadvantage of coming from the antipodes has to be suffered. But the political systems of our respective countries, including the office of Attorney General, are substantially similar. Moreover, as is evident from what I have written, I have studied this topic extensively and reflected on the various aspects of it at length. What I have to say may therefore be of some assistance. At least, that is my motivation and hope.

Areas of inquiry

I believe that there are a number of areas which the Committee will wish to probe.

Although at times phrased as questions, the following points are put forward as lines of inquiry. Naturally, I cannot anticipate the follow-up questions that the Committee will wish to pursue. Nor can I anticipate the questions which will arise out of the documentary material and testimony that will be available to the Committee. I appreciate, therefore, that the following points can do no more than provide a starting point.

One further point might be considered. Although I apprehend that the Committee members propose to question witnesses themselves, it may well be that this particular aspect, impregnated as it is with constitutional and legal issues, would benefit by having counsel appointed to assist the Committee. Such an appointment would not mean, of course, that Committee members would be precluded or inhibited from asking questions themselves. Counsel assisting an inquiry invariably occupy a subsidiary role. Such an appointment would simply mean that answers given by Lord Goldsmith, and possibly others within the Attorney General's office, which might appear acceptable and even persuasive, would be fully tested. I would emphasise that I am not suggesting that counsel be appointed generally or that the suggestion implies any lack of confidence in the Committee. Rather, after a lifetime in the law, I am impressed by the ingenuity of lawyers to proffer seemingly plausible answers which, certainly at times, only other lawyers succeed in unravelling.

(1) Political interference

A key question will be whether there was any 'political' interference or attempted interference with the Attorney General, or the office of the Attorney General, prior to Lord Goldsmith giving his formal opinion of 7 March 2003 and his advice given ten days later on 17 March 2003 and, if so, the nature and extent of that interference. This question strikes at the heart of the independence of the Attorney General. If that independence has been compromised, the nature and extent to which it has been compromised will need to be fully reported.

For this purpose, it will be important to ascertain whether the Attorney General had any discussions or communications relating to the legality of the war and the preparation and presentation of his opinion and advice with the Prime Minister, the Foreign Secretary, the Home Secretary, various Under-Secretaries, officials in the Prime Minister's Office or Foreign Office, and anyone purporting to represent or speak for those Ministers. If so, the timing and content of those discussions and communications will need to be examined.

This area of inquiry will be of particular importance in respect of any discussions or communications taking place in the ten days between the Attorney General's opinion of 7 March and his later advice of 17 March. It will be significant to ascertain whether any discussions of communications which took place in this ten day period drew the Attorney General's attention to the consequences for the Prime Minister, the Government or the military if an opinion from the Attorney General that the war was legal was not forthcoming.

The Attorney General will also need to be asked when he became aware that the Prime Minister and Cabinet were considering, or were seriously considering, whether or not to join in the invasion of Iraq.

Further, was the Attorney General aware that the Prime Minister had, contrary to the Ministerial Code of Conduct, advised Cabinet that '[T]he time to debate the legal basis for our action should be when we take that action' (Robin Cook, *The Point of Departure: Diaries from the Front Bench,* Pocket Books 2004, p 135). The Attorney General should be pressed as to whether he considers that he, as the Attorney General, had a responsibility to object to, or protest against, this delay or to otherwise draw attention to the fact that the Prime Minister's statement was contrary to the Ministerial Code of Conduct.

(2) The preparation of the Attorney General's opinion and advice

It will need to be ascertained whether and to what extent the Attorney General's advice of 17 March as to the legality of the war differed from opinions given from within the Attorney General's office and the Foreign Office and, if there were differences, how those differences were resolved (if they were resolved) and whether any such differences were made known to the Prime Minister and Cabinet.

The Foreign Office Deputy Legal Adviser, Ms Elizabeth Wilmshurst, sought early retirement or resignation in protest against the Attorney General's advice of 17 March. Was the Attorney General aware of her action and was he involved in any discussions about her decision?

It will also need to be known whether the Attorney General referred to outside sources for opinions as to the legality of the war and, if so, who were the sources and what were the opinions or advice received? My long experience in practice has revealed the unpalatable fact that persons seeking an 'independent' opinion are sometimes prone to select a barrister or legal academic whose disposition or approach are known in advance. I am not suggesting that the resulting opinion will not be overtly independent. It is likely, however, to reflect the known disposition or approach of the person providing the opinion. Much can also depend on how the question or instructions are framed. The opinion may be constrained or directed by the terms of the question posed or the instructions given.

The Attorney General might also be asked whether he resiles from his opinion given in his formal opinion of 7 March that 'aggression is a crime recognised by the common law which can be prosecuted in the UK courts'. (See memorandum from the Attorney General to the Prime Minister, 7 March, 2003, para 34). If, as is to be expected, the Attorney General does not resile from that opinion, he may properly be asked whether he considered his advice of 17 March exposed the Prime Minister and members of Cabinet to a prosecution should the war be held illegal. Further, did he advise the Prime Minister or Cabinet of this possibility when giving his advice of 17 March endorsing the legality of the war?

Under section 1 of the Law Officers Act 1997 the duties of the Attorney General can be delegated to the Solicitor General. The question therefore arises whether, having regard to the conflict of interest inherent in the office of Attorney General, Lord Goldsmith considered requesting an opinion from the Solicitor General as to the legality of the proposed invasion of Iraq. If not, the Attorney General could be asked why he did not do so.

(3) The critical ten days

Although judicial experience mandates an almost continuous state of uncertainty, I entertain not a scrap of doubt that some discussion or communication or event occurred after the Attorney General's opinion dated 7 March and before his subsequent advice of 17 March to change his opinion. I cannot accept, and I do not believe any judge would accept, that Lord Goldsmith's change of heart reached in ten short days was simply the outcome of further reflection or research. It defies belief. (See also Lord Lester QC's comment reported in the *Guardian* on 28 April 2005 under the heading, 'The Document and What it Means' quoted in *Spokesman 95* at p 31.)

It is to be recognized that the possible ramifications of an adverse opinion from the Attorney General just days before the planned invasion would have led to an almost unimaginable situation. I wish to quote a paragraph from my article on the independence of the Attorney General (July (2009) *New Zealand Law Journal*, at p 215):

> What would the military's response have been if it had not received the unequivocal assurance it sought that the war would be legal? Would it have been prepared to join the invasion set to take place just a few days later? Would

some Cabinet Ministers have resigned if the legality of the war had not been verified? Would there have been a second and more effective rebellion of Labour back-benchers without that advice? Would public opinion in the United Kingdom, already lukewarm if not opposed to the war, have become inflammably hostile? Even though the Bush Administration had made it clear that the United States would, if necessary, go it alone, what effect would an opinion from the Attorney General of Great Britain that the war would be in violation of international law have had on public support for the invasion in that country? What effect would it have had on one or more countries in the so-called coalition of the willing? The pressure on the Attorney General not to throw a spoke in the wheel must have been unimaginably enormous.

I do not believe that I am going too far or stepping out of line to say that the Committee's final report will be met with widespread scepticism if it cannot provide a plausible explanation for the shift in the Attorney General's opinion in these ten days. Political expediency is a credible explanation, but political expediency is incompatible with the role and responsibility of the Attorney General. Indeed, political expediency is the antithesis of that office.

Finally, Hans Blix's third and final report was published on 7 March (ten days before the Attorney General's advice of 17 March). In essence, the Report denied that it could be said Iraq was in substantial non-compliance with the resolutions of the United Nations and claimed that there was no evidence to the contrary. Was the Attorney General aware of this Report? If so, why did he not have regard to it in giving his advice of 17 March? Did he not consider that it contradicted the Prime Minister's view? If the Attorney General was not aware of the Report it is difficult to see how he could explain why it was not drawn to his attention or why he did not ask for and seek the most up to date evidence available.

(4) The publication of the advice of 17 March

The Attorney General's formal opinion of 7 March remained confidential for about 18 months before part of it was leaked. The Prime Minister then released the whole of the opinion a week before polling day. It is relevant to ask whether the Attorney General had any part in (1) the decision to retain confidentiality for his formal opinion until part of it was leaked, (2) the decision to leak part of the opinion 18 months later and, if so, what part was to be leaked, and (3) the subsequent decision to publish the full opinion.

The Prime Minister repeatedly claimed that the advice of 17 March was a précis or 'fair summary' of the Attorney General's opinion of 7 March.

He claimed that any suggestion 'that the legal opinion of the Attorney General was different from the Attorney General's statement to the House' was 'patently absurd', or words to that effect. The Committee could usefully explore whether the Attorney General accepts that his advice of 17 March was a 'précis' or 'fair summary' of his earlier opinion. Follow up questions, if the Attorney General makes that claim, would be to inquire of the respects in which his advice of 17 March is such a 'précis' or 'fair summary'. It is difficult to see how under moderate questioning the Attorney General would be able to maintain that position.

Questions might also be put to the Attorney General seeking to ascertain whether he thought that, as the Attorney General, he had an obligation or responsibility to clarify to the Cabinet and Parliament, and to the public, that his advice of 17 March was not a 'précis' or 'fair summary' of his opinion of 7 March.

A related inquiry would be to ascertain the Attorney General's knowledge of what material was put before Cabinet. At the very least it needs to be known whether the Attorney General was aware that Cabinet had not been informed of the reservations and qualifications in his formal opinion of 7 March. If he knew this to be the case, did he not accept that, as Attorney General, he had a responsibility to assure that his full opinion was put before Cabinet?

It is certain that the advice of 17 March was either put before Cabinet or known to Ministers. It is therefore relevant to ascertain whether Lord Goldsmith considered that he had a responsibility to ensure Cabinet was informed that his advice of 17 March had been preceded by a formal opinion just ten days earlier to a different effect.

Further, was the Attorney General aware that having his advice of 17 March only put before Cabinet was in breach of the Ministerial Code of Conduct which stipulates that full legal advice must be disclosed to Ministers whenever they are presented with a summarized version of the advice? (Ministerial Code of Conduct, para. 23)

(5) Validity of the Attorney General's advice

Particular attention will need to be given to the view of the Attorney General that it was open to the United Kingdom to undertake an invasion of Iraq in order to unilaterally enforce resolutions of the United Nations. In other words, what is the legal basis for the Attorney General's opinion that the United Kingdom could take military action in respect of a perceived breach of resolutions of the United Nations? Does the Attorney General consider that it would have been lawful for another country, say,

Iran or Turkey, to take military action against Iraq to enforce a resolution of the United Nations?

In particular, having said in his opinion dated 7 March that the United Kingdom's view of the revival argument was that only the Security Council could decide if a violation was sufficiently serious to revive the authorisation to use force, what occurred to lead the Attorney General to accept ten days later that this argument could be met by permitting the Prime Minister *alone* to decide that critical question?

The Prime Minister is recorded as having informed the Attorney General in writing that it was his 'unequivocal view' that Iraq was 'in further material breach' of its obligations to the United Nations. Did this letter include any supporting evidence? Did the Attorney General discuss the issue with the Prime Minister either before or after that letter? Did the Attorney General seek confirmation from the Prime Minister in writing that Iraq was in material breach of the resolutions of the Security Council? Did the Attorney General take any steps to institute a procedure or process to verify the Prime Minister's view? Did the Attorney General have any reservations about relying on the Prime Minister's view without further or official verification, particularly having unequivocally said in his opinion of 7 March that 'strong factual grounds' and 'hard evidence' would be required to justify military intervention? Why, too, did he not persist with the claim that legal authority would be contingent on the existence of weapons of mass destruction?

Indeed, the question could be usefully explored as to why the Attorney General thought that the question whether there had been a material breach of the resolutions of the United Nations was a matter that could be determined by 'evidence' from the Prime Minister at all. What, for example, would the Attorney General have said if the Security Council had concurrently expressly ruled that Iraq was not in material breach of the earlier resolutions? Would he have accepted the 'evidence' of the Prime Minister ahead of the Security Council? In fact, the Attorney General was correct in the first place. The decision was one for the Security Council to make, but if (as is denied) that decision could be made by an individual state it could only be made on the basis of a complete and objective analysis of all the available evidence.

The question is also pertinent as to why, in accepting the Prime Minister's view that Iraq was in further material breach of the resolutions of the United Nations, the Attorney General did not have regard to, or sufficient regard to, the reports of Hans Blix, the head of the United Nation's Monitoring, Verification and Inspection Commission, or

Mohammed ElBaradei, the Director-General of the International Atomic Energy Agency.

Again, did the Attorney General take any steps to ascertain the views of the Joint Intelligence Committee before accepting that Iraq was in further material breach of the resolutions of the United Nations?

In a statement on September 2004 Mr Kofi Annan, the Secretary-General of the United Nations, publicly stated that the war was illegal. Did this opinion cause the Attorney General to reconsider his advice of 17 March or take any steps to apprise the Prime Minster or Cabinet of the Secretary-General's opinion?

Finally, under this heading, I believe that it would be relevant to ask the Attorney General whether he is aware of the recently expressed view of Lord Bingham of Cornhill in his Grotius lecture to the British Institute of International and Comparative Law that the invasion of Iraq was 'a serious violation of international law and of the rule of law', (July (2009) *New Zealand Law Review*, at pp 214 and 216). Does he accept that this view is correct? If not, in what respects does he assert that Lord Bingham is in error?

Lord Bingham's lecture highlights the significance of various Articles in the Charter of the United Nations. I referred to a number of these in my article relating to the independence of the Attorney General in New Zealand (See July (2009) *New Zealand Law Review*, at pp 214-215). The Attorney General could be usefully asked whether he had regard to these Articles, or the effect of these Articles, in arriving at his view as to the legality of the war and, if so, why there is no reference to them in either his formal opinion of 7 March or his advice of 17 March. In this regard it may be noted by the Committee that in Library Research Paper 65/09 ((May 2009) entitled 'The Attorney General for England and Wales' Lord Goldsmith is reported to have identified, as the first of three specific elements in upholding the rule of law, 'compliance with the law … that means domestic and international obligations'. (See ibid, under the heading, 'A Guardian of the Rule of Law' at p 2).

The assembling of evidence – some comments

The answers to many of these questions will be clarified when the Committee obtains access to the relevant Cabinet papers and minutes, minutes or notes of Cabinet Ministers at the relevant meetings, and minutes or notes of meetings between the Prime Minister or the Prime Minister's advisers and the Attorney General, internal notes in the possession of the office of Attorney General and minutes or notes in the possession of the Foreign Secretary and the Foreign Office. This written record will, of course, be supplemented by the evidence given by the Prime

Minister, the Attorney General, the Foreign Secretary, the Foreign Office, key advisers, and other government officials to the Committee. I can add little to what I anticipate will be an exhaustive search and analysis of all the documentary material that will be available.

I would reiterate, however, that it would be of interest to establish in detail the occasions, both formal and informal, when the Attorney General met with the Prime Minister or the Prime Minister's advisers in the lead up to the war. As indicated above, specific attention would need to be given to any meetings or communications on or about 7 March and up to 17 March.

I imagine that Ms Elisabeth Wilmshurst will be called as a witness. A retirement or resignation of this kind over the advice given to the Government by the Attorney General was a remarkable development. Differences of opinion on legal issues are not uncommon but do not ordinarily give rise to a person resigning or threatening to resign. Ms Wilmshurst's stand is an indication that the Attorney General's advice was outside the bounds of legitimate differences of opinion. I think it highly probable that Ms Wilmshurst's views were shared by a number of other officials in the Foreign Office. It will be important to inspect the internal documents of the Office, more particularly as those officials who shared her view, but did not resign, may unconsciously and understandably defend their decision by crediting the Attorney General's advice with greater validity than they were prepared to concede at the time.

It is commonplace in an inquiry of this kind for the commission or committee of inquiry to concentrate on senior officials. But I suspect that a more complete picture of the background to the Attorney General's advice and the tension it must have created could be obtained by interviewing the more junior officials in the Attorney General's office and the Foreign Office who would have been caught up in the day to day events as they unfolded.

Although many of the areas of inquiry suggested above would tend to confirm that the invasion of Iraq was illegal, I am not certain that the Committee will be prepared to advance a definitive opinion as to the legality of the war. If it is of a mind to address that question, I would suggest that the view of Lord Bingham of Cornhill in his Grotius Lecture referred to above is an authoritative statement with which all or most judges and lawyers would agree. Although it is entirely a matter for the Committee, my own inclination would be to find that some issues are beyond doubt, such as the question whether it was open to the United Kingdom to seek to enforce a resolution of the United Nations and whether it was sufficient for the Attorney General to rely on the advice of the Prime Minister alone that Iraq was in material breach of the resolutions of that body. Other points may be said, perhaps, to be arguable. But I acknowledge that this suggestion may be regarded as unduly cautious.

In any event, the process by which the Attorney General arrived at his opinion of 7 March and advice of 17 March will still require attention. Apart from establishing the essential facts I would suggest, for example, that any competent judge or senior counsel would be able to advise the Committee on the legal differences between the Attorney General's opinion of 7 March and his advice of 17 March. The differences need to be tabulated.

Before leaving this topic I wish to emphasise the important distinction which exists between the question of the validity of the so-called revival argument and the question of the legality of the United Kingdom's action in seeking to take advantage of that argument. The question whether a breach of Resolution 1441 revived the earlier resolutions so that it was open to the Security Council to determine that action was required to enforce the earlier resolutions is logically distinct from the question whether it was open to the United Kingdom to lawfully determine that the earlier resolutions were revived and itself take action based on those resolutions. It may be acknowledged that there are lawyers who hold that the authority to use force contained in resolutions relating to the first Gulf War were revived if Iraq was in material breach of those resolutions. But I am not aware of any legal opinion, and certainly not any respectable legal opinion, where the determination that there had been a material breach could be taken by any body other than the Security Council or acted upon by any body other than the United Nations.

Possible reforms

I do not know how far the Committee will wish to go in recommending changes in the system to ensure that the advice a government receives from the Attorney General relating to possible military action is independent, and seen to be independent. The office of Attorney General is inherently political. It occupies a schizophrenic constitutional role as I have stressed in my article relating to the independence of that office as referred to above (July (2009) *New Zealand Law Review*).

The office of Attorney General dates back to the 13th century. Until late in the 19th century, the Attorney General's function was to represent the Crown in the courts. In 1673 the Attorney General officially became the Crown's adviser, but the Attorney General nevertheless continued to focus on litigation involving the Crown rather than giving advice to the Crown or government. It was only in the beginning of the 20th century that the focus of the Attorney General's role shifted to legal advice. Litigation involving the Crown was delegated to the Treasury Solicitors and Crown Prosecution Service.

It will at once be apparent that having responsibility for the conduct of litigation did not burden the Attorney General or his or her office with the same dual loyalties that attached to that office when the Attorney General became responsible for providing the government with legal advice. Consequently, the conflict between the Attorney General's function of advising the government and his or her obligation to be strictly independent has only become acute in the last century. It is probable that the problems inherent in this schizophrenic situation are only now being manifest.

Because of this long history and its constitutional importance, however, I anticipate that the Committee may wish to be circumspect in making recommendations relating to the status, office and role of the Attorney General. If, however, the Committee's findings confirm my own conclusions, the Committee may wish to consider a number of possible reforms. Again, I do not claim that the following suggestions are exhaustive. Further, some may overlap and become unnecessary if other suggestions are to find favour.

(1) Ensuring contestability

The fact that, constitutionally, the Attorney General is the legal adviser to the government of the day does not mean that his or her legal advice should necessarily prevail or that it should not be questioned. Few other institutions would be prepared to rest a major and serious decision on one legal opinion. Apart from the practice of obtaining second opinions on difficult questions, a basic feature of the legal system is that legal arguments are contested. Commerce has its own imperative, certainly at board level, in requiring executive decisions and recommendations to be contestable. In the medical profession second opinions are obtained as a matter of good medical practice in any difficult or serious case and, although at times a medical case may give rise to a question of life or death, the decision cannot be equated with a decision to take a country to war. The process should be no less rigorous in the governmental or political sphere.

Indeed, it is odd that, while the rest of the community take appropriate steps to ensure that they act upon the best legal advice when confronted with a difficult, serious or costly issue, a government may feel competent to undertake a war in which lives will be lost and many people will endure irreparable harm and suffering on the basis of one opinion as to its legality. It is nothing short of bizarre when the advice that the country is legally justified in going to war takes up little more than one side of a piece of A4 paper. No barrister or lawyer worth his or her salt would ever consider that such abrupt and skimpy treatment of an issue as serious as military action came close to meeting the long-standing standards the legal profession has set in providing opinions as to the law or to the public's expectation of the profession in that regard.

It is my respectful submission that the Committee should seek to ensure that nothing as cursory as the process followed on this occasion, accepted by the Attorney General as adequate, will ever happen again. On such matters as the legality of an invasion the Attorney General's advice should be tested. There is no reason why the issue, together with the Attorney General's opinion or advice, should not be referred to the Solicitor General for an opinion. Alternatively, there are any numbers of competent barristers and legal academics specialised in the field of law in question who could provide an independent opinion. Other means of ensuring that the Attorney General's advice is tested no doubt exist.

In summary, the United Kingdom undertook a war on the basis of advice from the Attorney General which was obtained and given far too late; which was astonishingly skimpy; which was substantively defective; which was inconsistent with a more formal opinion given only ten days earlier; which rested on the view of the Prime Minister that Iraq was in material breach of resolutions of the Security Council; which was contrary to the Report of the United Nation's own Inspector and the later opinion of the Secretary General; which followed a formal opinion that was not made known to the Cabinet or Parliament and which was kept confidential from the public; which was then misrepresented as a 'précis' or 'fair summary' of the earlier formal opinion; and which did not accord with the Ministerial Code of Conduct. Bluntly put, it was a charade, and I respectfully urge that the Committee ensure that its like never happens again.

(2) Separation of the office of Attorney General from the political process

Because of its historical and traditional role, it is unlikely that there will be much support for abolishing the office of Attorney General altogether. The office of Attorney General, however, could be divorced from the political and parliamentary process. This separation between the political process and officers exercising a legal function has occurred in other areas of government. The Committee will be aware that in 2005, as a result of the

Constitutional Reform Act of that year, the Lord Chancellor's dual roles as member of the government and the head of the judiciary in England and Wales and presiding officer of the House of Lords when exercising its judicial function as Lords of Appeal in Ordinary were brought to an end. The Lord Chancellor remains responsible for the functioning of the judiciary and the independence of the courts, but the notion that a serving politician appointed by the Sovereign on the advice of the Prime Minister should also hold a high judicial post and exercise a judicial function was rejected. The judicial functions were transferred to the Lord Chief Justice and Lord Speaker respectively.

By virtue of the same Act, the judicial function of the House of Lords was terminated and became the responsibility of the new Supreme Court of the United Kingdom. As the Committee will be aware, the Supreme Court commenced its work on 1 October 2009 in premises separate from the Houses of Parliament. Although their Lordships sitting as Lords of Appeal in Ordinary have never been influenced by their position as peers located in Westminster, that position was seen to be constitutionally unsound.

The separation of the office of Attorney General from the political and parliamentary process would be in line with these reforms. The Attorney General would remain the nominal head of the profession with responsibility for the judicial and legal process, but he or she would not be a member of the Houses of Parliament. He or she would advise the government of the day if and when consulted. They would attend Cabinet meetings only by invitation in respect of particular matters on which their advice is sought.

(3) Independent appointment of the Attorney General

At present, the Attorney General is appointed by the Sovereign on the recommendation of the Prime Minister. When the Attorney General is called upon to advise on issues as important as the legality of military action or on matters which may be politically embarrassing to the Prime Minister or the government, this method of appointment is undesirable. The United Kingdom has recently appointed an independent Judicial Appointments Commission which selects candidates for judicial office in courts and tribunals, mainly in England and Wales. Selection of these judicial officers was taken out of the hands of the Lord Chancellor. It was intended that the appointment process would be more clearly independent, transparent and accountable.

I envisage that this body, or a similar body, could be charged with the responsibility of appointing the Attorney General or making recommendations as to the appointment of the Attorney General.

(4) Express certification of independence

The Attorney General could be required to explicitly state at the close of his or her opinions or advice that he or she had not been subject to any outside influence or attempted influence. They could also be required to stipulate the meetings, discussions and communications which they have had in being briefed to give their opinion or advice. There is, indeed, no sound reason why the Attorney General should not be required to list the names of Ministers and officials with whom he or she has conferred prior to giving the opinion and specify the dates and times of those meetings, discussions or communications and the text of the question posed or instructions given in requesting the opinion or advice.

In short, the Attorney General could be required to append to his or her opinion or advice an express affirmation that they had acted independently and to provide sufficient information to allay any disquiet that he or she may not have been strictly independent.

(5) Amendments to the Ministerial Code of Conduct

Depending on its findings, the Committee may also consider that it would be prudent to explore the ways in which the temptation for politicians to influence the decision or opinion of the Attorney General could be inhibited. An appropriately worded amendment to the Ministerial Code of Conduct could seek to constrain the Ministers, including the Prime Minister, from attempting to influence any legal opinion or advice sought by the Minister or Cabinet.

A second amendment to the Ministerial Code of Conduct could reinforce the requirement that the Attorney General's opinion be obtained at the earliest possible time and that, other than in exceptional cases, the opinion be made immediately available to Ministers and Cabinet.

A third amendment to the Code could require that, again other than in exceptional circumstances, the Attorney General's opinion be made public within a certain time after the opinion has been given. Allowance must be made for exceptional circumstances, such as state security, where the withholding of an opinion or advice could be justified. But I would submit that, as a general rule, the principle of confidentiality should not attach to the Attorney General's legal advice. The argument that confidentiality should attach to the advice of officials to their Ministers so that their advice will be free, frank and unfettered does not apply, or apply with the same force, to the advice of the Attorney General. That officer required to give independent and objective advice as to the legal position and uphold the rule of law.

This line of thinking finds a measure of support in the Sixth Sir David Williams Lecture, 'The Rule of Law', given by Lord Bingham of Cornhill. Lord Bingham questions whether the ordinary rules of client professional privilege, appropriate enough in other circumstances, should apply to a law officer's opinion on the lawfulness of war. He expresses the view that it is not unrealistic to regard the public, those who are to fight and perhaps die, rather than the government, as the client. An opinion on the lawfulness of war, being the ultimate exercise of sovereign power involving the whole people, he believes, is quite different from situations where the ordinary rules of client professional privilege would apply. He adds that the case for full contemporaneous disclosure would seem to be even stronger when the Attorney General is a peer and not susceptible to direct questioning in the chamber.

An amendment requiring the Attorney General's opinion, other than in exceptional circumstances, to be a matter of public record within a fixed time would be consistent with this approach.

Conclusion

I express the hope that my submission, including the fact that I am making a submission from outside the boundaries of the United Kingdom, will not be seen as presumptuous. The importance of the issues which the Committee confronts extends well beyond its borders.

The independence of the Attorney General is of critical constitutional importance. If the Attorney General is not strictly independent, and does not act independently of the government of the day, the validity and value of the legal advice given by the Attorney General is, at the very least, suspect. The policy and decision-making process is then basically flawed. Public confidence in the political and legal systems is impaired and democracy is diminished. Importantly, the rule of law, and the democratic aspiration for a world order based on that precept, is in danger of being undermined.

Nothing less, therefore, than resolute independence will preserve the integrity and legitimacy of the office of Attorney General. In my submission, the Attorney General, Lord Goldsmith, did not demonstrate the requisite independence in the lead up to the war in Iraq. I would respectfully urge that it is incumbent on the Committee to spell out the role and culpability of the Attorney General and recommend the ways in which any possible dereliction of duty can be avoided in the future.

Parade of the Old New

I stood on a hill and I saw the Old approaching, but it came as the New.

It hobbled up on new crutches which no one had ever seen before and stank of new smells of decay which no one had ever smelt before.

The stone that rolled past was the newest invention and the screams of the gorillas drumming on their chests set up to be the newest musical composition.

Everywhere you could see open graves standing empty as the New advanced on the capital.

Round about stood such as inspired terror, shouting: Here comes the New, it's all new, salute the new, be new like us! And those who heard, heard nothing but their shouts, but those who saw, saw such as were not shouting.

So the Old strode in disguised as the New, but it brought the New with it in its triumphal procession and presented it as the Old.

The New went fettered and in rags; they revealed its splendid limbs.

And the procession moved through the night, but what they thought was the light of dawn was the light of fires in the sky. And the cry: Here comes the New, it's new, salute the New, be new like us! would have been easier to hear if all had not been drowned in a thunder of guns.

Bertolt Brecht
From *The Darkest Times*
1938-1941

Another Agenda

Bob Marshall-Andrews MP

The author has provided penetrating analysis of the Iraq Inquiry under Sir John Chilcot ever since it was announced (see Spokesman 105). Here he reflects on Tony Blair's testimony to the Inquiry on 29 January 2010.

None of the members of the Chilcot Inquiry have training in either legal principles or forensic skills. They have no permanent appointed legal experts or advisers and no appointed counsel to represent the tribunal and to cross-examine witnesses. This was quite deliberate. The government that set up this Inquiry was quite open on the subject. It was widely suggested by the prime minister and others that the presence of skilled cross-examiners would conceal rather than reveal the truth. To this patent nonsense was added the issue of expense. The Iraq war has to date cost £26,000,000,000. Appointing a legal team to assist the Inquiry, would be, it was maintained, prohibitively expensive.

There was, of course, another agenda. In assessing responsibility for the Iraq disaster, past and present members of this government are the prime suspects. Although the Inquiry is famously not 'a court', its public purpose is to reveal the manifest deceptions and concealments that led us to participate in a conflict that caused massive suffering, the loss of 600,000 lives and a huge increase in fundamentalism and terror. Most prime suspects for most crimes or misdemeanours would opt for a trial without a skilled prosecutor and preferably with unqualified judges. And that's what the government achieved.

The extent to which the prime suspect, Tony Blair, was consulted or complicit in the shaping the process is, of course, unknown, but, whether by accident or design, he has precisely the tribunal he would have devised. An Inquiry has been created that is devoid of the forensic tools properly to enquire. It is a tribunal without teeth providing trial without tribulation.

And, of course, evidence is not on oath.

The results were predictable. In the main areas of controversy the Inquiry has proved itself totally ill-equipped to test or challenge testimony which demands the most rigorous and forensic examination. In doing so it has failed lamentably to investigate deceptions of Parliament, and in particular the central issue of the Attorney General's legal advice to Cabinet and Westminster. In terms of importance this issue has no equal. If Cabinet or Parliament had been told, or believed, that the legal case for war was doubtful, there would have been no war. If it now transpires that Parliament or Cabinet had been deceived or misled on this issue, the effect would resonate across the whole investigation, and would illuminate the extent to which we had secretly been committed to war at the behest of an American machine. Legality is the issue in its own right, and is the prime test of the integrity and bona fides of the architects of war.

The facts themselves are well known and stark. After months in which he had maintained that only a further UN resolution could legitimise war, the Attorney General partially changed his mind. He produced, on 7 March 2003, a written opinion for the Prime Minister. In it he acknowledged that a 'reasonable case' could be made for legality without the UN resolution but (and it is of course a huge 'but') he 'could not be confident that this view would succeed in a court of law'. In other words, put plainly, legality was doubtful.

The effect of this was potentially seismic. Had this view been known to the Cabinet or Parliament, votes for the war would have been unthinkable. Had this unvarnished view been known to our military command and armed forces, many, if not all, would have refused to fight. Had it been known to contractors, civil servants and unions engaged on war work many, if not all, would have withdrawn their labour and support.

At this point 40,000 British troops were massed on the borders of Iraq and war was three weeks away. On 17 March the Attorney General attended Cabinet. The purpose of his attendance was to provide his opinion that the war was legal. His own doubts and equivocations 10 days earlier received no mention. As to the very existence of a written opinion, there was total silence. The following day he repeated his unequivocal view on the law to the House of Lords, whence it came to the Commons. As to the very existence of a written opinion there was, again, total silence.

The reason given for this extraordinary passage of events was, when it came, lame and unacceptable to any lawyer (or indeed anyone). The Attorney General effectively said that he had been approached by the Chief of the Defence Staff and a representative of the Cabinet Office asking that his advice be made unequivocal and he duly obliged.

This lamentable, inexcusable saga demanded from the Chilcot Inquiry searching, forensic analysis and penetrating, relentless enquiry. It received neither. Blair's main inquisitor, Sir Roderic Lyne, failed repeatedly to formulate the essential questions, did not pursue manifest evasion, and allowed interminable responses that steadily eroded the allotted time. It was dreadful.

He had begun badly. Lyne's first, rambling 'question' contained multiple strands and comments inviting a long rambling 'reply' during which Blair noticeably relaxed. This was going to be a cakewalk. Nearly six minutes of time (two per cent of the day's session) had been wasted, and we had discovered precisely nothing.

It got worse. Answer after answer descended into self-serving waffle of total irrelevance. His love of America, his closeness to President Clinton, his admiration for the armed forces, the indescribable nastiness of Saddam, 'the calculus of risk' (what?), his experience as a junior barrister, even his silly asides to Fern Britton expanded endlessly to suffocate meaning. No one demanded a straight answer. No one deplored the obvious strategy of delay.

In the morass, essential questions surfaced briefly, were avoided and remained, amazingly, ignored. Question: 'Had President Chirac phoned to say that his position was being misrepresented out of context? Answer: 'I remember speaking to Chirac on a number of occasions.' Yes? And? What is the answer? We will never know as the examination drifted gently on to another topic, and obscurity remained.

Essential issues – the detailed conversations with Bush, the exact undertakings given by Blair on military support, the Downing Street memo, all surfaced briefly, were evaded ('Look, what I think needs to be made absolutely clear, Sir Roderic ...'), and then drifted harmlessly away.

Then came legality. Here, surely, lay the killer punch – the line of cross-examination that was essential, and from which there appeared no conceivable escape. It was, like the best cross-examination, so simple. 'Why was the Cabinet and Parliament kept in ignorance of the existence (never mind the content) of the Attorney General's only written opinion?' Why did Prime Minister and Attorney General watch their colleagues vote for a 'legal' war without mentioning once the existence of written advice given days before that legality was uncertain? Why? Tell us.

We will not know the answer for one simple reason. The question was never asked. Why was it never asked? Ask the Chilcot inquiry. See if you get an answer.

With grateful acknowledgements to the author for his permission to reprint this article, and to The Guardian, *where it was published online on 31 January 2010.*

Demockracy

Bob Dixon

April 23rd, St George's Day, saw the biggest non-
demonstration that London had never seen.

About two million people didn't march
and didn't carry banners proclaiming:
    WE WANT WAR!
and   KILL ALL THE BLOODY FOREIGNERS!
The fascist banners were nowhere, neither saying,
    KEEP BRITAIN WHITE!
nor   IF THEY'RE BLACK
    SEND THEM BACK.
Other banners didn't say,
    POLLUTION IS FUN
    FUCK THE FISH!
nor did they say,
    MAKE WAR, NOT LOVE!

Many of those who didn't march
Hadn't made their own placards.
One didn't say:
    ACTUALLY, I LIKE SEEING FOXES
    TORN TO PIECES ALIVE, ACTUALLY
and another didn't say:
    MAKE BRITAIN GREAT AGAIN
    BRING BACK THE THUMBSCREW, THE RACK,
    THE BIRCH AND THE NOOSE
Another didn't say:
    SEND BACK BOGUS ASYLUM SPONGERS AND
    SCROUNGERS AND TERRORISTS MILKING THE
    SYSTEM SWAMPING BRITISH CULTURE AND
    LIVING ON HAND-OUTS FROM BRITISH
    TAX-PAYERS IN LUXURY COUNCIL FLATS
    AND HOLIDAY CAMPS WITH FREE HEALTH
    CARE AND EDUCATION IN SPECIAL SCHOOLS

As the throng didn't move along Piccadilly,
their silent chants
didn't bounce off the façades
of the huge buildings.
We didn't hear:
> *What do we want?*
> *Blood!*
> *When do we want it?*
> *Now!*
nor:
> *One two three four*
> *give us war give us war*
> *two four six eight*
> *love is dead give us hate*
Nobody was stirred by this non-demonstration.

The prime minister, however, heeded their
  silent protest,
noted their absence from the lobbies
and lack of petitions and letters
and promised to give an ear to their unvoiced cries
– in the interests of demockracy.

Bob Dixon died in 2008. We are grateful to his publishers, Artery Publications, for permission to reprint this poem from Make Capitalism History: Poems and Other Communications. *More of Bob's poems will be read at a Poetry and Music Evening in Solidarity with Venezuela at the Embassy's cultural venue at Bolivar Hall (nr. Warren St. station) on 16 April at 7.00pm.*

Britain can't handle the truth

Scott Ritter

The author was a senior UN arms inspector in Iraq for eight years to 1998. He is the author of Iraq Confidential: The untold story of America's intelligence conspiracy *(I B Tauris Publishers).*

With its troops no longer engaged in military operations inside Iraq, Britain has been liberated politically to conduct a post-mortem of that conflict, including the sensitive issue of the primary justification used by then Prime Minister, Tony Blair, for going to war, namely Iraqi weapons of mass destruction, or WMD.

The failure to find any weapons of mass destruction in Iraq, following the March 2003 invasion and subsequent occupation of that country by US and British troops, continues to haunt those who were involved in making the decision for war. The issue of Iraqi weapons of mass destruction, and the role it played in influencing the decision for war, is at the centre of the ongoing Iraq war inquiry being conducted by Sir John Chilcot.

Among the more compelling testimonies provided to date has been that of Sir Christopher Meyer, the former British Ambassador to the United States who served in that capacity during the lead-up to the invasion of Iraq. Meyer convincingly portrayed an environment where the decision by the US to invade Iraq, backed by Blair, precluded any process (such as viable UN weapons inspections) that sought to compel Iraq to prove it had no WMD. Rather, Britain and the US were left 'scrambling' to find evidence of a 'smoking gun' to prove Iraq indeed possessed the weapons of mass destruction it was accused of having.

In short, Saddam had been found guilty of possessing weapons of mass destruction, and his sentence had been passed down by Washington and London void of any hard evidence that such weapons, or even related programmes, even existed. The sentence meted out – regime termination – mandated such a massive deployment of troops and material that all but the wilfully blind or intentionally ignorant had to know by the early autumn of 2002 that war with Iraq was inevitable. One simply does not initiate the movement of hundreds of thousands of troops, thousands of armoured vehicles and aircraft, and dozens of ships on a whim or to reinforce an idle threat.

President George Bush was able to disguise his blatant militarism behind the false sincerity of his ally Blair and his own secretary of state, Colin Powell. The President's task was made far easier given the role of useful idiot played by much of the mainstream media in the US and Britain, where reporters and editors alike dutifully repeated both the hyped-up charges levied against Iraq and the false pretensions that a diplomatic solution was being sought.

The tragic final act of the farce directed by Bush and Blair was the theatre of war justification known as UN weapons inspections. Having played the weapons of mass destruction card so forcefully in an effort to justify war with Iraq, the US (and by extension, Britain) were compelled once again to revisit the issue of disarmament. But the reality was that disarming Iraq was the furthest thing from the mind of either Bush or Blair. The decision to use military force to overthrow Saddam was made by these two leaders independent of any proof that Iraq was in possession of weapons of mass destruction. Having found Iraq guilty, the last thing those who were positioning themselves for war wanted was to re-engage a process that not only had failed to uncover any evidence of Iraq's retention of weapons of mass destruction in the past, but was actually positioned to produce fact-based evidence that would either contradict or significantly weaken the case for war already endorsed by Bush and Blair.

The US and Britain had both abandoned aggressive UN weapons inspections in the spring of 1998. UN weapons inspectors were able and willing to conduct intrusive no-notice inspections of any site inside Iraq, including those associated with the Iraqi president, if it furthered their mandate of disarmament. But the US viewed such inspections as useful only in so far as they either manufactured a crisis that produced justification for military intervention (as was the case with inspections in March and December 1998), or sustained the notion of continued Iraqi non-compliance so as to justify the continuation of economic sanctions. An inspection process that diluted arguments of Iraq's continued retention of weapons of mass destruction by failing to uncover any hard evidence that would sustain such allegations, or worse, sustain Iraq's contention that it had no such weaponry, was not in the interest of US policy objectives that sought regime change, and as such required the continuation of stringent economic sanctions linked to Iraq's disarmament obligation.

The British were never willing (or able) to confront meaningfully the American policy of abusing the legitimate inspection-based mandate of the UN inspectors. Instead, London sought to manage inspection-based confrontation by insisting that before any intrusive inspection could be carried out, it would have to be backed by high-quality intelligence. But even this position collapsed in the face of an American decision, made in April 1998, to stop supporting aggressive inspections altogether.

In the end, the British were left with the role of fabricating legitimacy for an American policy of terminating weapons inspections in Iraq, supplying dated intelligence of questionable veracity about a secret weapons cache being stored in the basement of a Ba'ath party headquarters in Baghdad, which was used to trigger an inspection the US hoped the Iraqis would balk at. When the Iraqis (as hoped) balked, the US ordered the inspectors out of Iraq, leading to the initiation of Operation Desert Fox, a 72-hour bombing campaign designed to ensure that Iraq would not allow the return of UN inspectors, effectively keeping UN sanctions 'frozen' in place.

As of December 1998, both the US and Britain knew there was no 'smoking gun' in Iraq that could prove that Saddam's government was retaining or reconstituting a weapons of mass destruction capability. Nothing transpired between that time and when the decision was made in 2002 to invade Iraq that fundamentally altered that basic picture.

But having decided on war using weapons of mass destruction as the justification, both the US and Britain began the process of fabricating a case after the fact. Lacking new intelligence data on Iraqi weapons of mass destruction, both nations resorted to either recycling old charges that had been disproved by UN inspectors in the past, or fabricating new charges that would not withstand even the most cursory of investigations.

The reintroduction of UN weapons inspectors into Iraq in November 2002 was counterproductive for those who were using weapons of mass destruction as an excuse for war. This was aptly demonstrated when, in the first weeks following their return to Iraq, the inspectors discredited almost all of the intelligence-based charges both the US and Britain had levelled against Iraq, while failing to uncover any evidence of the massive stockpile of weapons of mass destruction that Iraq had been accused of retaining.

The decision for war had been made independently of any viable intelligence information on Iraqi weapons of mass destruction. As such, the work of the UN weapons inspectors inside Iraq following their return in November 2002 was not a factor in influencing the lead-up to the actual invasion of Iraq. Having decided that Saddam was guilty of possessing weapons of mass destruction, the failure of the UN weapons inspectors to uncover evidence of such retention made their efforts not only irrelevant, but undesirable. The inconvenience of the UN weapons inspectors when it comes to the truth about the lead-up to the war with Iraq continues to this day.

The parade of British diplomats and officials appearing before the Chilcot hearings rightly point out the absolute lack of any 'smoking gun' concerning Iraq and weapons of mass destruction. But until Chilcot receives testimony from those best positioned to speak about Iraq's weapons of mass destruction programmes, namely the UN weapons inspectors themselves, all the hearings will succeed in doing is sustain the false appearance of well-meaning British officials, stampeded into a war with Iraq by an overbearing American ally, looking in vain for a 'smoking gun' that would justify their decision to invade. The evidence needed to undermine any weapons of mass destruction-based case for war, derived from the work of the UN weapons inspectors, was always available to those officials in a position to weigh in on this matter, but either never consulted or deliberately ignored.

There is a big difference between searching for a 'smoking gun' and searching for the truth. By ignoring and/or undermining the work of the UN weapons inspectors in the lead-up to the war with Iraq, British officials demonstrated that they were not interested in the truth about Iraqi weapons of mass destruction, a fact that testimony provided by the likes of Sir Christopher Meyer alludes to, but falls short of actually stating.

The search for truth can be an inconvenient process, especially when it threatens to expose potentially illegal activities in the prosecution of an unpopular war. Until he calls upon UN weapons inspectors themselves to deliver testimony before his inquiry, Sir John Chilcot perpetuates the perception that Britain simply can't handle the truth when it comes to uncovering the level of official British culpability in the deliberate fabrication of a case for war against Iraq that everyone knew, or should have known, was false.

With grateful acknowledgements to the author for his permission and to The Guardian, *where this article appeared on 27 November 2009.*

Writing Principia

Bertrand Russell

Betrand Russell founded The Spokesman.

A conference celebrating 100 years of Principia Mathematica, *entitled PM@100, will take place at McMaster University in Ontario, Canada from 21 to 24 May 2010, organised by the University's Bertrand Russell Research Centre. Details are available online (pm100.mcmaster.ca).*

In 1910, following years of intensive effort, Bertrand Russell embarked on the publication, with Cambridge University Press, of Principia Mathematica, *which was to become a landmark study in the foundation of mathematics. On 15 November, in a letter to Helen Flexner, a relative by marriage who taught English at Bryn Mawr College in Pennsylvania, he wrote:*

> *'The first volume of the big book that Whitehead and I have been engaged on for the last 10 years is going to appear in a few weeks ... This will be a great event in my life.'*

To mark the centenary of this momentous event, we reprint a small selection from Russell's own writings. There is Russell's affectionate pen portrait of Alfred North Whitehead, his collaborator on Principia, *which was published in* Portraits from Memory. *And, to set the scene, there is a short excerpt from Russell's* Autobiography.

* * *

In 1905 things began to improve. Alys and I decided to live near Oxford, and built ourselves a house in Bagley Wood. (At that time there was no other house there.) We went to live there in the spring of 1905, and very shortly after we had moved in I discovered my Theory of Descriptions, which was the first step towards overcoming the difficulties which had baffled me for so long. Immediately after this came the death of Theodore Davies ... In 1906 I discovered the Theory of Types. After this it only remained to write the book out. Whitehead's teaching work left him not enough leisure for this mechanical job. I worked at it from ten to twelve hours a day for about eight months in the year, from 1907 to 1910. The manuscript became more and more vast, and every time that I went out for a walk I used to be afraid that the house would catch fire and the manuscript get burnt up. It was not, of course, the sort of manuscript that could be typed, or even copied. When we finally took it to the University Press, it was so large that we had to hire an old four-wheeler for the purpose. Even then our difficulties were not at an end. The University Press estimated that there would be a loss of £600 on the book, and while the syndics were willing to bear a loss of £300, they did not feel that they could go above this figure. The Royal Society very generously contributed £200, and the remaining £100 we had to find ourselves. We thus earned minus £50 each by ten years' work. This beats the record of *Paradise Lost*.

Autobiography

* * *

Alfred North Whitehead

My first contact with Whitehead, or rather with his father, was in 1877. I had been told that the earth is round, but trusting to the evidence of the senses, I refused to believe it. The vicar of the parish, who happened to be Whitehead's father, was called in to persuade me. Clerical authority so far prevailed as to make me think an experimental test worth while, and I started to dig a hole in the hopes of emerging at the antipodes. When they told me this was useless, my doubts revived.

I had no further contact with Whitehead until the year 1890 when as a Freshman at Cambridge, I attended his lectures on statics. He told the class to study article 35 in the textbook. Then he turned to me and said, 'You needn't study it, because you know it already'. I had quoted it by number in the scholarship examination ten months earlier. He won my heart by remembering this fact. His kindness did not end there. On the basis of the scholarship examination he told all the cleverest undergraduates to look out for me, so that within a week I had made the acquaintance of all of them and many of them became my lifelong friends.

Throughout the gradual transition from a student to an independent writer, I profited by Whitehead's guidance. The turning-point was my fellowship dissertation in 1895. I went to see him the day before the result was announced and he criticized my work somewhat severely, though quite justly. I was very crestfallen and decided to go away from Cambridge without waiting for the announcement next day. (I changed my mind, however, when James Ward praised my dissertation.) After I knew that I had been elected to a fellowship, Mrs Whitehead took him to task for the severity of his criticism, but he defended himself by saying that it was the last time that he would be able to speak to me as a pupil. When, in 1900, I began to have ideas of my own, I had the good fortune to persuade him that they were not without value. This was the basis of our ten years collaboration on a big book no part of which is wholly due to either.

In England, Whitehead was regarded only as a mathematician, and it was left to America to discover him as a philosopher. He and I disagreed in philosophy, so that collaboration was no longer possible, and after he went to America I naturally saw much less of him. We began to drift apart during the First World War when he completely disagreed with my pacifist position. In our differences on this subject he was more tolerant than I was, and it was much more my fault than his that these differences caused a diminution in the closeness of our friendship.

In the last months of the war his younger son, who was only just eighteen, was killed. This was an appalling grief to him, and it was only by an immense effort of moral discipline that he was able to go on with his work. The pain of this loss had a great deal to do with turning his thoughts to philosophy and with causing him to seek ways of escaping from belief in a merely mechanistic universe. His philosophy was very obscure, and there was much in it that I never succeeded in understanding. He had always had a leaning toward Kant, of whom I thought ill, and when he began to develop his own philosophy he was considerably influenced by Bergson. He was impressed by the aspect of unity in the universe, and considered that it is only through this aspect that scientific inferences can be justified. My temperament led me in the opposite direction, but I doubt whether pure reason could have decided which of us was more nearly in the right. Those who prefer his outlook might say that while he aimed at bringing comfort to plain people I aimed at bringing discomfort to philosophers; one who favoured my outlook might retort that while he pleased the philosophers, I amused the plain people. However that may be, we went our separate ways, though affection survived to the last.

Whitehead was a man of extraordinarily wide interests, and his knowledge of history used to amaze me. At one time I discovered by chance that he was using that very serious and rather out-of-the-way work, Paolo Sarpi's *History of the Council of Trent,* as a bed book. Whatever historical subjects came up he could always supply some illuminating fact, such, for example, as the connection of Burke's political opinions with his interests in the City, and the relation of the Hussite heresy to the Bohemian silver mines. No one ever mentioned this to me again until a few years ago, when I was sent a learned monograph on the subject. I had no idea where Whitehead had got his information. But I have lately learnt from Mr John Kennair Peel that Whitehead's information probably came from Count Lützow's *Bohemia: an historical sketch.* Whitehead had delightful humour and great gentleness. When I was an undergraduate he was given the nickname of 'the Cherub', which those who knew him in later life would think unduly disrespectful, but which at the time suited him. His family came from Kent and had been clergymen ever since about the time of the landing of St. Augustine in that county. In a book by Lucien Price recording his dialogues in America, Whitehead describes the prevalence of smuggling in the Isle of Thanet at the beginning of the nineteenth century when brandy and wine used to be hidden in the vaults of the church with the approbation of the vicar: 'And more than once,' he remarked, 'when word was brought during service that officers were coming up the road, the whole congregation adjourned to get that liquor out of the way assisted by the vicar. That is evidence of how intimately the Established Church shares the life of the nation.' The Isle of Thanet dominated the Whitehead that I knew. His grandfather had migrated to it from the Isle of Sheppey and, according to Whitehead, was said by his friends to have composed a hymn containing the following sublime stanza:

> Lord of the Lambkin and the Lion,
> Lord of Jerusalem and Mount Zion,
> Lord of the Comet and the Planet,
> Lord of Sheppey and the Isle of Thanet!

I am glad that my first meeting with him was in the Isle of Thanet, for that region had a much more intimate place in his make-up than Cambridge ever had. I felt that Lucien Price's book ought to be called *Whitehead in Partibus,* 'Partibus' being not everything outside England, but everything outside the Isle of Thanet.

He used to relate with amusement that my grandfather, who was much exercised by the spread of Roman Catholicism, adjured Whitehead's sister never to desert the Church of England. What amused him was that the contingency was so very improbable. Whitehead's theological opinions were not orthodox, but something of the vicarage atmosphere remained in his ways of feeling and came out in his later philosophical writings.

He was a very modest man, and his most extreme boast was that he did try to have the qualities of his defects. He never minded telling stories against himself. There were two old ladies in Cambridge who were sisters and whose manners suggested that they came straight out of *Cranford*. They were, in fact, advanced and even daring in their opinions, and were in the forefront of every movement of reform. Whitehead used to relate somewhat ruefully, how when he first met them he was misled by their exterior and thought it would be fun to shock them a little. But when he advanced some slightly radical opinion they said, 'Oh, Mr. Whitehead, we are so pleased to hear you say that', showing that they had hitherto viewed him as a pillar of reaction.

His capacity for concentration on work was quite extraordinary. One hot summer's day, when I was staying with him at Grantchester, our friend Crompton Davies arrived and I took him into the garden to say how-do-you-do to his host. Whitehead was sitting writing mathematics. Davies and I stood in front of him at a distance of no more than a yard and watched him covering page after page with symbols. He never saw us, and after a time we went away with a feeling of awe.

Those who knew Whitehead well became aware of many things in him which did not appear in more casual contacts. Socially he appeared kindly, rational, and imperturbable, but he was not in fact imperturbable, and was certainly not that inhuman monster 'the rational man'. His devotion to his wife and his children was profound and passionate. He was at all times deeply aware of the importance of religion. As a young man, he was all but converted to Roman Catholicism by the influence of Cardinal Newman. His later philosophy gave him some part of what he wanted from religion. Like other men who lead extremely disciplined lives, he was liable to distressing soliloquies, and when he thought he was alone he would mutter abuse of himself for his supposed shortcomings. The early years of his marriage were much clouded by financial anxieties, but, although he found this very difficult to bear, he never let it turn him aside from work that was important but not lucrative.

He had practical abilities which at the time when I knew him best did not find very much scope. He had a kind of shrewdness which was surprising and which enabled him to get his way on committees in a manner astonishing to those who thought of him as wholly abstract and unworldly. He might have been an able administrator but for one defect, which was a complete inability to answer letters. I once wrote a letter to him on a mathematical point, as to which I urgently needed an answer for an article I was writing against Poincaré. He did not answer, so I wrote again. He still did not answer, so I telegraphed. As he was still silent, I sent a reply-paid telegram. But in the end, I had to travel down to Broadstairs to get the answer. His friends gradually got to know this peculiarity, and on the rare occasions when any of them got a letter from him they would all assemble to congratulate the recipient. He justified himself by saying that if he answered letters, he would have no time for original work. I think the justification was complete and unanswerable.

Whitehead was extraordinarily perfect as a teacher. He took a personal interest in those with whom he had to deal and knew both their strong and their weak points. He would elicit from a pupil the best of which a pupil was capable. He was never repressive, or sarcastic, or superior, or any of the things that inferior teachers like to be. I think that in all the abler young men with whom he came in contact he inspired, as he did in me, a very real and lasting affection.

Portraits from Memory

May Day Greetings!

Build Peace not Bombs

Bob Crow
General Secretary

Alex Gordon
President

Kurt is up in heaven now

Kurt Vonnegut

Kurt Vonnegut's first near-death experience was an accident, during a hospital operation that went wrong. He then planned another 'in cooperation with Dr Jack Kevorkian and the staff at the state-of-the-art lethal injection execution facility at Huntsville, Texas'. He followed this with a series of 90-second broadcasts for New York City's public radio station, WNYC, as the station's 'reporter on the afterlife' who interviewed more than 20 people at the end of the 'blue tunnel to the Pearly Gates'. We reproduce three of these, with John Brown, Clarence Darrow, and Eugene Victor Debs.

… I am honory president of the American Humanist Association, having succeeded the late, great, spectacularly prolific writer and scientist, Dr. Isaac Asimov in that essentially functionless capacity. At an AHA memorial service for my predecessor I said, 'Isaac is up in Heaven now.' That was the funniest thing I could have said to an audience of humanists. It rolled them in the aisles. Mirth! Several minutes had to pass before something resembling solemnity could be restored.

I made that joke, of course, before my first near-death experience – the accidental one.

So when my own time comes to join the choir invisible or whatever, God forbid, I hope someone will say, 'He's up in Heaven now.' Who really knows? I could have dreamed all this …

* * *

Today's controlled near-death experience was a real honey! I interviewed John Brown – whose body lies a-moulderin' in the grave, but whose truth goes marchin' on. One hundred forty years ago, come October 2, he was hanged for treason against the United States of America. At the head of a force of only eighteen other anti-slavery fanatics, he captured the virtually unguarded Federal Armory at Harper's Ferry, Virginia. His plan? To pass out weapons to slaves, so they could overthrow their masters. Suicide.

Law-abiding citizens opened fire from all sides, killing eight of his men, two of them his sons. He himself was taken prisoner by a force of United States Marines, sworn to uphold the Constitution.

Their commander was Colonel Robert E. Lee.

John Brown wears a hangman's noose for a necktie up in Heaven. I asked him about it, and he said, 'Where's yours? Where's yours?'

His eyes were like glowing coins. 'Without shedding of blood,' he said, 'there is no remission of sin.' It turns out that's in the New Testament, Hebrews 9:22.

I congratulated him on what he'd said on his way to be hanged before a gleeful, jeering throng of white folks. I quote: 'This is a beautiful country.' In only five words, he had somehow encapsulated the full horror of the most hideous legal atrocities committed by a civilized nation until the Holocaust.

'Slavery was legal under American law,' he said.

'The Holocaust was legal under German law,' he said.

John Brown is a Connecticut Yankee, born in Torrington. He said there was a Virginian, Thomas Jefferson, who had actually encapsulated God in only six words: 'All men are created equal.'

Brown was twenty when Jefferson died. 'This perfect gentleman, sophisticated, scientific, wise,' John Brown went on, 'was able to write those incomparable sacred words while owning slaves. Tell me: Am I really the only person to realize that he, by his example, made our beautiful country an evil society from the very first, where subservience of persons of color to white people was deemed in perfect harmony with natural law?'

'I want to get this straight,' I said. 'Are you saying that Thomas Jefferson, possibly our country's most beloved founding father, after George Washington, was an evil man?'

'Let that, while my body lies a-molderin' in the grave,' said John Brown, 'be my truth which goes marchin' on.'

(Choral rendition of one stanza of 'Battle Hymn of the Republic.')

This is Kurt Vonnegut, signing off in the lethal injections facility at Huntsville, Texas. Until next time, ta ta.

* * *

Dr. Jack Kevorkian has again unstrapped me from what has become my personal gurney, here, in the lethal injection facility at Huntsville, Texas. Jack has now supervised fifteen controlled near-death experiences for me. Hey, Jack, way to go! On this morning's trip down the blue tunnel to the pearly gates, Clarence Darrow, the great American defense attorney, dead for sixty years now, came looking for me. He wanted WNYC's listeners to hear his opinions of television cameras in courtrooms. 'I welcome them,' he said, if you can believe it. This man with the reputation of a giant, comes from a rinky dink little farm town in Ohio.

'The presence of those cameras finally acknowledges,' he said to me, 'that justice systems anywhere, anytime, have never cared whether justice was achieved or not. Like Roman games, justice systems are ways for unjust governments – and there is no other sort of government – to be enormously entertaining with real lives at stake.'

I thanked Mr. Darrow for having made American history much more humane than it would have been otherwise, with his eloquent defenses in court of early organizers of labor unions, of teachers of unpopular scientific truths, and for his vociferous contempt for racism, and for his loathing of the death penalty. And the late, great lawyer Clarence Darrow said only this to me: 'I did my best to entertain.'

Signing off now. Hey, Jack, waddaya say we go downtown for some of that good old Tex-Mex cuisine?

*   *   *

During what has been almost a year of interviewing completely dead people, while only half dead myself, I asked Saint Peter again and again if I could meet a particular hero of mine. He is my fellow Hoosier, the late Eugene Victor Debs of Terre Haute, Indiana. He was five times the Socialist Party's candidate for president back when this country still had a strong Socialist Party.

And then, guess what, yesterday afternoon none other than Eugene Victor Debs, organizer and leader of the first successful strike against a major American industry, the railroads, was waiting for me at the far end of the blue tunnel. We hadn't met before. This great American died in 1926 at the age of seventy-one when I was only four years old.

I thanked him for words of his, which I quote again and again in lectures: 'As long as there is a lower class, I am in it. As long as there is a criminal element, I am of it. As long as there is a soul in prison, I am not free.'

He asked me how those words were received here on Earth in America nowadays. I said they were ridiculed. 'People snicker and snort,' I said. He asked what our fastest growing industry was. 'The building of prisons,' I said.

'What a shame,' he said. And then he asked me how the Sermon on the Mount was going over these days. And then he spread his wings and flew away.

*   *   *

Farewell Michael Foot

Michael Foot has died, well into his nineties. Some years ago, in 1998, he introduced a new edition of Bertrand Russell's Autobiography *with these words:*

'A particular, persistent reason why Bertrand Russell had such appeal throughout his ninety odd years, especially to the young, was the trouble he took to write plain English.'

Foot went on to praise what he regarded as 'one of the truly great autobiographies in our language'. Another of Foot's favourite writers of plain and potent English was Thomas Paine, who was his 'number one revolutionary hero'. By way of tribute to Michael Foot, we reprint a review he wrote of three works concerning Paine, which was probably Foot's last published work.

Just about 20 years ago, with Jill Craigie at the top of her intellectual form, when she thought the cinema could raise all the arts to a higher degree of excellence, we got the news from a good source that at last a proper film was to be made on a subject which cried out for it: Thomas Paine.

He had been my number one revolutionary hero and, instructed perhaps by her love of revolutions, Rebecca West, he was high up on Jill's list too. It so happens that we had been together with several Indian friends who knew that what we were seeing at the first-night showing of Richard Attenborough's *Ghandi* was the truly epic subject properly displayed.

The actors contributed to the film's success but it was the vision of the great director testing his new instruments to the limit which would achieve the great results. Not so long after that night of triumph we were told that Attenborough was turning his imaginative mind to Thomas Paine as his next great subject.

It could still happen, but meantime I must give readers an update on Thomas Paine matters. Some may recall that I have, on occasion, such is his important role in history, suggested changing the name of Trafalgar Square to Thomas Paine Square. It would be a nice compliment to the Americans and the French, since he played such an important part in achieving their freedom as well as ours.

However, I now report not the great film but three new books, which should remind us afresh how essential were the causes we honour today.

The first and the most significant is *These Are The Times: A Life of Thomas Paine* by Trevor Griffiths, who makes his dedication:

'For Richard Attenborough, comrade and conductor on this long march'. Such words might suggest that the march is ended, but not necessarily so. Here is the brilliant and truly original screenplay written by Griffiths for the film, and I hope that its publication may revive the idea of making it. Most of the scenes take place in America, but they speak again to the whole world.

Griffiths is a true Painite, and I was sent this copy by an old friend who also qualifies for that title, Ken Coates, of the Bertrand Russell Peace Foundation in Nottingham.

The second book, Bernard Vincent's *The Transatlantic Republican: Thomas Paine and the Age of Revolutions*, offers a series of fresh lectures and reviews. Vincent has already played a leading role in restoring Paine's proper reputation in France.

Paine himself never forgot his debt to the people of France and Paris in particular. But only with Vincent's scholarship and political insight has that association been properly restored. The other truly great contribution to this period was John Keane's book, *Tom Paine: A Political Life*, published by Bloomsbury on May 1, 1995. Never was there a better date to remind us of the even greater glory of July 14th which all those truly entitled to call themselves revolutionaries, the women even more than the men, must still celebrate. Keane then told the story better than ever before, and he would have been happy to acclaim those who are just catching up.

Third, Penguin has just published in its Great Ideas series, Thomas Paine's *Common Sense*, which first made him infamous. On December 3rd, the Thomas Paine Society held its annual meeting in London's Conway Hall, which is our regular meeting place. Without Conway Hall, without Moncure Conway, true revolutionaries of the modern age would have no such appropriate place to meet. Without his truly liberal ideas, embracing women as well as men, which he brought from America, we would still be living in the intellectual dark ages.

The more we look today on the persistent topicality of Paine's political ideas, the more we see for ourselves that it is the potency of his writing which prevails, and we may be all the more amazed to recall that Richard Carlile was imprisoned in 1823 for selling Paine's *Rights of Man*. Carlile concluded that matter thus: 'His pen continued an overmatch for the whole brood.'

Trevor Griffiths, These Are The Times – A Life of Thomas Paine, Spokesman Books, Bernard Vincent, The Transatlantic Republican – Thomas Paine and the Age of Revolutions, Amsterdam Monographs in American Studies, Editions Rodopi B.V. Thomas Paine, Common Sense, Penguin Books Great Ideas Series.

Judgment

The Rt Hon
the Lord Judge

The Rt Hon
the Lord Neuberger

*These excerpts are taken
from the two judgments of
the Court of Appeal when
it found for Binyam
Mohamed in an appeal
brought by the Secretary
of State for Foreign and
Commonwealth Affairs,
David Miliband, who had
challenged the publication
of written reports of Mr
Mohamed's torture at the
hands of US personnel.*

*David Miliband, the Foreign Secretary,
tried three times to claim Public Interest
Immunity, and prepared three separate
immunity certificates for the Court, in an
attempt to prevent publication of seven
paragraphs detailing what the British
Security Services knew about the torture of
Binyam Mohamed as a result of reports they
had received from US intelligence sources
in May 2002. But the Foreign Secretary's
claims were rejected by the Court on
grounds of genuine public interest in what
the paragraphs revealed about the
treatment of Mr Mohamed, and also
because of the unreliability of information
contained in the certificates which had been
supplied by the Security Services.*

*Once the Foreign Secretary had finally
accepted the judgment of the Court that the
world might know what tortures United
States personnel had been inflicting on
Binyam Mohamed, and in which the British
authorities were complicit, another storm
broke over Mr Miliband's head. The Master
of the Rolls, Lord Neuberger, had prepared
his draft judgment in Binyam Mohamed's
case, dated 10 February 2010. This
contained criticisms of the conduct of the
British Security Services. At a late hour,
paragraph 168 of the draft judgment was
challenged by a barrister acting for the
Foreign Office. This eventually caused the
High Court to publish a further judgment,
on 26 February 2010. Such a step, as the
Lord Chief Justice, Lord Judge, explains, is
'highly unusual'. We reprint excerpts from
this further judgment of the Lord Chief
Justice of England and Wales, the Master of
the Rolls, and the President of the Queen's
Bench Division between The Queen on the*

application of Binyam Mohamed and The Secretary of State for Foreign and Commonwealth affairs.

The Lord Chief Justice of England and Wales

1. This is the judgment of the court.
2. The circumstances in which it has become necessary to give a further judgment are highly unusual. In brief, the Secretary of State for Foreign and Commonwealth Affairs (the Foreign Secretary) appealed against the decision of the Divisional Court in the proceedings brought by Binyam Mohamed that seven redacted sub-paragraphs of its first judgment should be made public. The appeal was dismissed. Three separate judgments were given. Although the reasoning in these judgments was not identical, the emphasis of the Lord Chief Justice differing from that of the Master of the Rolls and the President of the Queen's Bench Division, the decision was unanimous. In total the judgments ran to 296 paragraphs. Unless the Foreign Secretary proposed a further appeal to the Supreme Court the litigation was at an end, and the redacted paragraphs could at long last be published.
3. The present judgment is concerned with one paragraph (paragraph 168) in the judgment of the Master of the Rolls. This paragraph has attracted huge public attention …

Lord Neuberger, Master of the Rolls

29. … the final version of paragraphs 168 to 170 in my judgment of 10th February 2010 is as follows:

'168. Fourthly, it is also germane that the Security Services had made it clear in March 2005, through a report from the Intelligence and Security Committee, that "they operated a culture that respected human rights and that coercive interrogation techniques were alien to the Services' general ethics, methodology and training" (paragraph 9 of the first judgment), indeed they "denied that [they] knew of any ill-treatment of detainees interviewed by them whilst detained by or on behalf of the [US] Government" (paragraph 44(ii) of the fourth judgment). Yet, in this case, that does not seem to have been true: as the evidence showed, some Security Services officials appear to have a dubious record relating to actual involvement, and frankness about any such involvement, with the mistreatment of Mr Mohamed when he was held at the behest of US officials. I have in mind in particular witness B, but the evidence in this case suggests that it is likely that there were others. The good faith of the Foreign Secretary is not in question, but he prepared the certificates partly, possibly largely, on the basis of information and advice provided by Security Services personnel. Regrettably, but inevitably, this must raise the question whether any statement in the certificates on an issue concerning the mistreatment of Mr Mohamed can be relied on, especially when the issue is whether contemporaneous communications to the Security Services about such mistreatment should be revealed publicly. Not only is there some reason for distrusting such a statement, given that it is based on Security Services' advice and information, because of previous, albeit general, assurances in 2005, but also the Security Services have an interest in the suppression of such information.

169. My concern on this point is mitigated by the fact that the certificates appear to be supported by communications from the US, most pertinently the CIA letter and what was recorded as having been said by the Secretary of State. The US Government, like any other Government, plainly has an interest in ensuring that it controls the flow of any information which it provides to the SyS [Security Services] on a confidential basis, and the fact that it (and other Governments) may well be motivated in this case by embarrassment is not the point: one is concerned with hard facts, not moral judgements.

170. My conclusion on this half of the balancing exercise is this. While there are strong reasons for scepticism, I accept that the Foreign Secretary genuinely believes, and has some grounds for believing, what he has stated in the three certificates, namely that the flow of information from foreign Government intelligence services to the SyS [Security Services] could be curtailed if the redacted paragraphs are published, because that publication would be regarded by those Governments as an unjustifiable breach of the control principle. The normal reasons for deferring to his views on such an issue are diluted by the fact that there is nothing inherently sensitive in the information in those paragraphs, the very narrow and technical nature of the breach, the fact that the US must have appreciated the risk of intelligence material being disclosed pursuant to the law, the fact that other material apparently subject to the control principle has been revealed in the first judgement without objection, and a concern which arises from the apparent involvement of at least one Security Services agent in the mistreatment of Mr Mohamed. However, it is right to weigh against these factors the fact that the Foreign Secretary's opinion is reinforced by the CIA letter and the notes of the views of the Secretary of State.'

Spooks sold down the river

Clive Stafford Smith

The author is Legal Director of Reprieve, an organisation based in London that upholds the human rights of prisoners, particularly those sentenced to death. He is admitted to practise law in the state of Louisiana and in Washington DC.

The past month has seen a parade of spies going public. Mostly, they seem intent on insisting how little they know about the terrible goings-on in the world.

First, it was the MI5 director general, Jonathan Evans, writing in the *Telegraph*. 'We did not practise mistreatment or torture then and do not do so now, nor do we collude in torture or encourage others to torture on our behalf.'

Then it was the turn of Evans' predecessor, Baroness Eliza Manningham-Buller. 'It wasn't actually until after I retired that I read that, in fact, [Khalid Shaikh Mohammed] had been waterboarded 160 times', she told a parliamentary meeting.

Evans carefully shifted tenses, and thereby said nothing that was remotely relevant to the pending criminal investigation. Nobody has ever intimated that the British tortured Binyam Mohamed. Rather, the allegation is that they stood by and watched while the Americans did the abuse. Evans carefully refrained from saying 'nor did we collude in torture' – because we did.

Likewise, Manningham-Buller said absolutely nothing of significance. We know she did not read about Khalid Shaikh Mohammed's waterboarding until after she left her job – she retired on 20 April, 2007, and the truth did not emerge until a year later. Nobody has ever made the remotest suggestion to the contrary: she set up a straw man and shoved him back down.

It is hardly surprising that the spooks are saying very little of relevance – that is in their nature. But why did they choose this moment to say very little so very loudly?

Our intelligence agents are not blind to

the obvious. Peering from their burrows like Punxsutawney Pete, they panicked. The cause of their dismay? The politicians – the only people who are revealing less about torture than the spies, albeit even more loudly.

Never did a team play for the final whistle more plainly than this government. If the ministers can get past a May election, the Labour realists expect to join Tony Blair on the lecture circuit, far from the perils of office. The thin red line of Labour optimists, afraid that the sins of their recent past could prove an electoral iceberg, pin their wavering hopes on a continued cover-up. They weave and dodge, dodge and weave. Their plan is simple: if they win the election, they will figure out another way to weave; if they lose, the Tories will be forced either to continue the dissimulation or, like President Obama, to shoulder blame for the wrongdoings of a predecessor.

The spooks are being sold down the river, and they know it. The torture scandal should have been long behind them. Had the politicians made a public acknowledgement – 'Regrettably, mistakes were made in the political tsunami that followed 9/11' – all would have rapidly been forgiven. Only the most sanctimonious media commentator would have been writing about it a fortnight later.

Richard Nixon taught the world the danger of the cover-up. The botched Watergate burglary was of minor significance; the White House conspiracy to keep it secret drove Nixon from office. It turned the word 'gate' into a suffix for every political evil. So now each day brings a further revelation in Torturegate. Jonathan Evans suggested in the *Telegraph* that 'an allegation has been made that one of my officers might have committed a criminal offence'. Unfortunately for Evans, the seeping evidence suggests that this is not the case. It may not have been 'my officer' who committed the offence, but Evans himself.

'My officer' was the whistleblower who reported seeing a British prisoner being abused by the Americans on 10 January 2002 – and asked what he should do. It was very likely Evans – in charge of counter-terrorism at the time, and presumably working closely with his boss, Manningham-Buller – who sent back a telegram the next day, advising the agent that if he witnessed torture taking place in front of him, he could legitimately ignore it, given that the prisoner was in American custody. The police are not just investigating the small fry, but those responsible for the crimes as well.

Of course, we might have had sympathy for Evans and Manningham-Buller, as they were responding in the wake of 9/11, perhaps the most televised mass crime in history. But the political cover-up has eroded this sympathy. Rather than a frank admission, and an open apology, the original crime has been compounded by the subsequent dissembling.

Friday 12 March 2010 brought the latest bad news, when the Intelligence and Security Committee (ISC) released its 2009 report. Referring to evidence of abuse that had been hidden from it in the Binyam Mohamed case, the Committee noted that it had only recently learned 'that at least four members of staff saw the information, including the team leader … and their section head'. So five more members of MI5 will be drawn into the pending criminal investigation.

'The allegations of collusion in torture and the lack of respect for human rights will wound [MI5 agents] personally and collectively, and … will make it harder for them to do their jobs,' said Manningham-Buller. But the problem is not the allegation of complicity, but the fact that the allegations have been proven true time and time again – against a background of concerted government obfuscation.

The next government must order a full and independent inquiry. Nobody who is forthright about his mistakes should be sent to jail. The process should be conducted in a spirit of honesty and reconciliation, for we can only learn from history if we know what that history was. Then, when the next inevitable crisis comes, we may hope to respond with greater wisdom. If, on the other hand, officials continue to dissemble, we will still be wading through this mire for many years to come.

With grateful acknowledgements to the author for his permission, and to The Independent on Sunday, *where this article appeared on 14 March 2010.*

* * *

The Chilcot Enquiry
(Three haiku questions)

After the Iraq
invasion comes the Whitehall
whitewash – why so bland?

Seven years too late,
which sop will soothe a public
still concerned with truth?

When slimy creatures
wriggle, sliding off the hook
as always – what's new?

Alexis Lykiard

Carnage in Gaza

Nurit Peled Elhanan

The author teaches at the University of Tel Aviv, in which city she spoke at a protest rally to mark the first anniversary of the Israeli Defence Force's assault on Gaza, named Operation Cast Lead, that began on 27 December 2008. More than 1,400 Palestinians were killed during the 22 days of assault by land, air and sea. She is also a founder of the Russell Tribunal on Palestine, which met for its opening session in Barcelona in March 2010 (see report below).

We mark the first anniversary of the carnage in Gaza, and protest at the comfortable complacency which inhabitants of this city and this country exhibit before the slow annihilation that goes on and on in Gaza and throughout Palestine.

Had Israeli pre-school children been asked 'what did you learn at school this year, dear little boy of mine?', there are all kinds of answers that we might have received. An enlightened and critical child might have answered: I learned that the sun is still shining, and the almond tree is blooming, and the butcher butchers, and there is nobody to judge him.[1]

And the child who is less used to theorizing might rejoice and say: I learned how to cheat Americans, deceive Palestinians, kill Arabs, expel families from their homes, and to curse whoever tells me that I am a nasty brat when I have been a nasty brat. And I learned that the Jewish People lives, and that Gilad Shalit [held captive by Hamas] also lives. Still.[2]

And the new immigrant boy, who longs terribly to integrate and belong, might say: I learned whom to hate, I learned who needs to be killed and who should be spat upon, and I am ever ready for the task, whenever you call upon me.

The Religious-Zionist child, who attends the fenced and well-guarded kindergarten in the settlement, might say: I learned to be a good Zionist, to love the Land, to die and kill for its sake, to expel from it the invaders, to kill their children, to destroy their homes, and never to forget that in each and every generation the persecutors arise to annihilate us, and that all gentiles are the same, and that they are all anti-semites who must be annihilated. And the most important is that the sun is still shining, and the almond tree is still blooming, and soon we will go planting all over the mountains of Samaria and Judea, and guard well the saplings against the herd of sheep which invaded our country in the two thousand years that we have not been here to guard it.

In the past year our children have learned that to kill a non-Jew, of whatever age, is a great commandment. This they learned not only from the rabbis, but also from the soldiers who ceaselessly boast of what they have done. This was expressed well by Damian Kirilik, when the police arrested him and charged him with murdering the entire Oshrenko family.[3] Quite coolly, he asked the police investigators: 'why are you making such a fuss over the killing of children?' Damian Kirilik is a new immigrant who does not understand the nuances and sophistry of the rabbis' command to kill gentile children. But this assassin from the outside quickly got the general idea – he had arrived at a place where the murder of children is taken very lightly.

Our children have learned this year that all the disgusting qualities which anti-semites attribute to Jews are actually manifested among our leaders: deceit and deception, greed, and the murder of children. While accused of trading in transplanted organs, the unperturbed Government of Israel is engaged in trading in whole humans – for the time being. It can be conjectured that, for years to come, when many cars would bear the bumper sticker 'Gil'ad – born to be free'[4], the captains of the pirate ship known as Israel will continue their scheming and haggle over how many kilograms of Jewish flesh, which is probably shrinking, could be traded for how much Palestinian flesh, which is also not all that it used to be, as we learned from the news item about theft of skin and corneas at the Abu Kabir Forensic Center.[5] And they will continue to kill in Gil'ad's name, and starve and suffocate in Gil'ad's name, to annihilate the Palestinian people slowly but surely and, on the way, encourage the flourishing of the Palestinian bad 'weeds'[6] that always legitimize the ongoing killing.

As in every rotten and corrupt society, the word 'values' recurs again and again in every speech of every politician, especially the wanted ones. The values of Zionism and the values of Judaism and the values of the Israeli Defence Force. The values of Zionism we have seen this year in their full glory at the expulsion of families from their homes in Sheikh Jarrah. The values of Democracy and the Rule of Law are expressed in Palestinians, who are suspected of a violent act, being extra-judicially assassinated in their homes, in front of their children, while Jewish terrorists enjoy to the full the amenities of the judicial system.

That is what our children learn in the Jewish democratic state. Therefore, one can wonder at the supposed shock expressed in the face of violence in schools and nightclubs, in streets and on the roads. After all, this violence is nothing but practising the values of the Israeli Defence Force, a course of basic training towards the activities and operations waiting for these youths on their horizon. This is these youths' way of showing that they have learned something from their parents and elder brothers, from their teachers and guides. The only problem which apparently disturbs the educational and law enforcement authorities is that there are no Palestinians in the Jewish schools and the Jewish night clubs and the Jewish streets. For lack of them, the young Jews direct their violence at each other – and that should not happen, a Jew should not harm another Jew. Violence should be disciplined and regulated, guided by blind obedience to the racial laws, directed only and solely at those who are not Jewish.

And we who demonstrate every week, every month, at every carnage, at every anniversary of a carnage – what is our power? Nothing. Bereavement and failure is our lot in this country. Recently, we all stood at the gates of Gaza, disciplined and obedient to the conditions of the police permit, happy to see each other and find out that we are still alive, and chanted slogans loudly at an audience of robot-like police and soldiers, totally incapable of comprehending what we had to say. But we did not pull down the wall. We did not succeed in saving even one child from the plague of meningitis which has infested Gaza for several months already.

What shall we do with our impotence and failure? What is left to be done about an educational system which demands of its graduates a total identification with Jewish guerrilla fighters who were, before 1948, executed by the British on charges of terrorism – and at the very same time a total identification with their executioners? To identify with the victims of Auschwitz, and at the same to behave with cruel indifference to the suffering of anyone who is not a member of our race? What can peace seekers do in a country which is run by the army, whose schools are infested with war criminals coming to instil their teachings, where pupils are obliged to experience a week in the pre-military Gadna (Youth Squads) and listen to heroic tales told by the criminals of the Gaza carnage, on whom all possible psychological and social and educational means are applied to make them part of the killing machine?

These are our sons and daughters – and we have no access to the system which guides their lives. Where is there space left for us to instil in them one or two of our own values? What values of beauty and goodness can we squeeze into such a sophisticated apparatus of brainwashing and reality distortion?

It seems that the only value which we still have the power and means to instil is the value of refusal – to learn to say 'no'. To teach our children who have not been poisoned yet to resist the brainwashing, to reject the viruses with which their brains are being injected. It is hard, a sisyphean task, but it is the only way to reassert our humanity. To say no to evil, no to deceit and deception, no to trade in human beings, no to the racism which is spreading over here like wildfire, a racism which does not stop at the Kalandia Checkpoint nor at the Erez Checkpoint, but spreads like cancer to the shameful immigrant absorption centres, to the schools which proclaim integration and practise segregation, to all cultures and all beliefs in this country. If we don't learn to refuse and reject evil, to refuse the evil laws and regulations, we will find ourselves refusing and rejecting ourselves, our inmost truth. We must refuse to feel ourselves an extinct minority, refuse the fear and apprehension – and the alienation – which are imposed on us, refuse to be accomplices. Only refusal can save us from surrender, from bankruptcy, from despair. We stand here today as an alien and alienated minority, hated and persecuted. But together with our peace-seeking friends beyond the Wall, beyond the barbed wires, we might become a majority. Only the refusal to surrender to walls and checkpoints can open the gates of our ghetto so that we could pull down the walls of their ghetto. To see at last that there is an outside world, that there are regions which the Jewish National Fund has not destroyed. That there is a culture and there are people whom it is worth living to meet, to know and make friends with, to learn from them about this place where we live as resident aliens, and remember that this place can be a place of surpassing beauty.[7]

Translated by Adam Keller

Notes compiled by the translator

References

1 A reference to Bialik's famous poem on the 1903 Kishinev Pogrom.
2 'Am Yisrael Hai' ('the Jewish People lives') – a traditional saying, often invoked in a nationalist context.
3 http://www.jpost.com/servlet/Satellite?cid=1256799068438&pagename=JPArticle%2FShowFull
4 The slogan 'Ron Arad – born to be free' refers to captured Israeli pilot Ron Arad,

for whose release the government in the 1990s refused to release Palestinian and Lebanese prisoners, and who is widely considered to be irretrievably lost.

5 See http://www.guardian.co.uk/world/2009/dec/21/israeli-pathologists-harvested-organs

6 Settler leaders dissociate themselves from extreme acts of violence against Palestinians, defining the perpetrators as 'the weeds in our garden'.

7 The Hebrew term used, 'Yefe Nof', is taken from the poem of longing for Jerusalem written by the Medieval Spanish Jewish poet Yehuda HaLevi: 'O Abode of Surpassing Beauty/Joy of the Entire Earth ...'

THE BERTRAND RUSSELL PEACE FOUNDATION
DOSSIER

2010   Number 33

Russell Tribunal on Palestine

The first session of The Russell Tribunal on Palestine (RTP) took place in Barcelona from 1 to 3 March 2010. It found European Union member states in breach of international and internal European Union law with respect to the protection of human rights of Palestinians. We will publish the session's full findings in a special Spokesman pamphlet. Meanwhile, here is a preliminary report of proceedings.

The session jury comprised eminent legal experts and human rights activists*. It heard testimony from international experts and witnesses on a range of issues. They include:
– the principle of respect for the right of the Palestinian people to self-determination;
– the settlements and the plundering of natural resources;
– the annexation of East Jerusalem;
– the blockade of Gaza and Operation Cast Lead;
– the construction of the Wall in the Occupied Palestinian Territory;
– the European Union/Israel Association Agreement.

The Tribunal found that Israel was violating the right of Palestinians to self-determination as enshrined in **The Declaration on the granting of independence to colonial countries and peoples** and all **United Nations General Assembly (NGA) resolutions** that have reaffirmed the right of the Palestinian people to self-determination since 1969. Furthermore, by occupying Palestinian territories since June 1967 and refusing to leave them, Israel violates the **Security Council resolutions** that demand its withdrawal from the territories concerned.

The Tribunal also found Israel's discriminatory acts towards Palestinian

---

*Jury members were Mairead Corrigan Maguire, Cynthia McKinney, Gisèle Halimi, Aminata Traore, Ronnie Kasrils, Alberto San Juan, Michael Mansfield, Arcadi Oliveres, Jose Antonio Martin Pallin.

populations inside Israeli territory and occupied Palestinian territory to be in violation of the **Convention on the Suppression and Punishment of the Crime of Apartheid of 18 July 1976**, which is not binding on Israel, though this does not exonerate Israel in such regard. The acts include closure of the borders of the Gaza Strip and restrictions on the freedom of movement of its inhabitants; preventing the return of Palestinian refugees to their home or land of origin; prohibition on the free use by Palestinians of certain natural resources such as watercourses within their land.

By annexing Jerusalem in July 1980, and maintaining the annexation, Israel violates the prohibition of the acquisition of territory by force, as stated by the **Security Council Resolution 478 of 20 August 1980.**

By constructing a Wall in the West Bank on Palestinian territory that it occupies, Israel denies the Palestinians access to their own land, violates their property rights, and seriously restricts the freedom of movement of the Palestinian population, thereby violating **article 12 of the International Covenant on Civil and Political rights** to which Israel became a party on 3 October 1991; the illegality of the construction of the Wall was confirmed by the **International Court of Justice in its Advisory Opinion of 9 July 2004,** which was endorsed by the **UN General Assembly.**

By systematically building settlements in Jerusalem and the West Bank, Israel breaches the rules of international humanitarian law governing occupation, in particular **article 49 of the Fourth General Convention of 12 August 1949,** by which Israel has been bound since **6 July 1951.** This point was noted by the International Court of Justice in the above-mentioned Advisory Opinion.

By pursuing a policy of targeted killings against Palestinians whom it describes as 'terrorists', without first attempting to arrest them, Israel violates the right to life of the persons concerned, a right enshrined in **article 6 of the Covenant on Civil and Political Rights 1966.**

By maintaining a blockade on the Gaza Strip, Israel breaches the provisions of the **Fourth Geneva Convention of 12 August 1949 (art. 33),** which prohibits collective punishment.

By inflicting extensive and serious damage, especially on persons and civilian property, and by using prohibited methods of combat during operation 'Cast Lead' in Gaza (December 2008 – January 2009) it committed further breaches.

European Union member states were found to be violating provisions of the **Lisbon Treaty** (2010) including foundational principles of the EU itself as set down in article 2, which confirms attachment 'to the values of respect for human dignity, freedom, democracy, equality, the rule of law and respect for human rights'.

European Union member states, as high contracting parties to the **Geneva Conventions 1949,** were found to be breaching elementary obligations of due diligence and ensurance of peremptory legal norms which cannot be derogated from, by failing to react to and remedy violations of the convention committed by Israel. As such they were found to be assisting Israel in its breaches of international law.

Article 146 compels EU member states 'to undertake to enact any legislation necessary to provide effective penal sanctions for persons committing, or ordering to be committed, any of the grave breaches of the present Convention defined in the following Article'.

Grave breaches include wilful killing, torture or inhuman treatment, including biological experiments, wilfully causing great suffering or serious injury to body or health, unlawful deportation or transfer or unlawful confinement of a protected person, compelling a protected person to serve in the forces of a hostile Power, or wilfully depriving a protected person of the rights of fair and regular trial and extensive destruction and appropriation of property, not justified by military necessity and carried out unlawfully and wantonly.

International Law Commission articles on state responsibility for wrongful acts were found to apply to EU member states, as is the **1966 Covenant on Civil and Political Rights,** which states:

'Every State has the duty to promote through joint and separate action universal respect for and observance of human rights and fundamental freedoms in accordance with the Charter.'

Reports from experts brought to light passive and active forms of assistance in the alleged commission of breaches by the European Union and its member states particularly through:

– exports of weapons and components of weapons by EU states to Israel, some of which were used during the conflict in Gaza in December 2008 and January 2009;
– exports of produce from settlements in occupied territories to the European Union;
– participation by the settlements in European research programmes;
– failure of the European Union to complain about the destruction by Israel of infrastructure in Gaza during Operation Cast Lead;
– failure of the European Union to demand Israeli compliance with clauses concerning respect for human rights contained in the various association agreements concluded by the EU with Israel;

– the decision by the European Union to upgrade its relations with Israel under the Euro-Mediterranean Partnership Agreement;

– tolerance by the European Union and its member states of certain economic relations between European companies and Israel involving commercial projects in the occupied territories, such as the management of the Tovlan landfill site in the Jordan valley and the construction of a tramline in East Jerusalem.

In conclusion of its first Barcelona session, the Russell Tribunal on Palestine calls on:

(i) the European Union and its member states to fulfil their obligations forthwith by rectifying the breaches specified in the final ruling;

(ii) the European Union in particular to implement the EU Parliament resolution requiring the suspension of the EU-Israel Association Agreement and thereby putting an end to the impunity that Israel has benefited from until now;

(iii) European Union member states to implement the recommendation at para 1975 (a) of the UN Fact Finding Mission Report on the Gaza Conflict (Goldstone Report) regarding the collection of evidence and the exercise of universal jurisdiction against Israeli and Palestinian suspects;

(iv) European Union Member states to repeal any requirements in any member state that a suspect must be a resident of that member state or of any impediments to the compliance with the duty to prosecute or extradite for trial all suspected war criminals sought out by member states.

(v) European Union member states to ensure that universal jurisdiction laws and procedures are made as effective as possible in practice, including through co-ordination and the implementation of agreements on the mutual co-operation of states on criminal matters, through the EU contact points on cross-border and international crime, EUROPOL and INTERPOL, etc.

(vi) European Union member states to make no regressive changes that would blunt the effect of existing Universal Jurisdiction laws, so as to ensure that no EU member state becomes a safe haven for suspected war criminals;

(vii) The Parliaments of Austria, France, Greece and Italy to pass laws providing the penal legislation required by article 146 of the Fourth Geneva Convention to enable universal jurisdiction to be exercised in those countries.

(viii) individuals, groups and organisations to take all avenues open to them to achieve compliance by EU member states and the European Union of their aforementioned obligations, as exemplified by the use of universal jurisdiction over individual criminal suspects, domestic civil proceedings against individual governments and/or their departments or agencies and private companies, in respect of which it is the intention of the Russell Tribunal on Palestine to commission and/or encourage others to commission research into which countries and jurisdictions these matters can most effectively be pursued; and

(ix) the existing legal actions and campaigns in the context of boycott, divestment and sanctions (BDS) to be stepped up and widened within the European Union and globally.

The Russell Tribunal on Palestine calls on the European Union and on each of its member states to impose the necessary sanctions on its partner Israel through diplomatic, trade and cultural measures in order to end the impunity that it has enjoyed for decades. Should the European Union lack the necessary courage to do so, the Tribunal counts on the citizens of Europe to bring the necessary pressure to bear on it by all appropriate means.

More information: www.russelltribunalonpalestine.net

John Smith by Ken Gill
(see page 94)

Reviews

Black Gold

David John Douglas, *Geordies – Wa Mental,* a revised edition of an earlier 2002 edition, published in 2008 by Read 'n' Noir, an imprint of Christie Books of Hastings, East Sussex, distributed by Central Books Ltd, 99 Wallis Road, London E9 5LN, 354 pages including end notes and a glossary, paperback ISBN 9781873976340, £9.99

This autobiography is described by the publisher as the first volume of a trilogy, *Stardust and Coaldust*, of which a second volume, *The Wheel's Still in Spin*, appeared in 2009 (to be reviewed later). The volume reviewed here describes the first 20 years of the life of David John Douglas (Dave), born in Tyneside in 1948 of loving parents – a caring Irish-Catholic mother and a thoughtful, tolerant, Methodist, mine-worker father.

David Douglas may not have intended it, but the story so far is of the 'radicalisation' (such a useful word these days) of a working class child. It started only gently at home with some verbal history of mineworker abuse over the ages, but mainly at school with endemic bullying by pupils and staff. Corporal punishment at school was routine, and expectations were low. In spite of all that, his humour is poignant, piercingly honest and irrepressible. You will laugh alright. How could the teachers cope when every child, even in the 1960s, had an inkpot in his or her desk.

Ink monitors, trusted clean kids, let loose on a galvie jug full of the stuff, trusted to its safe distribution. Little hands hold forth the pot as line by line the galvie jug lad walks down the isle, like a priest at communion. Tipping each in turn, until – until that evil temptation takes grip and the jug is tipped, the pot filled, overfilled, and the ink flows down the arms, over the bare leg down the shoe and into a pool on the wooden floor.

His religious education was intense to the point of destruction. When Mother had moved him to a Catholic school he learned the catechism.

'Who made you?
God made me.
Why did God make you?
God made me to know Him, love Him and serve Him in this world and for ever in the next.'

In the juniors each would sit carrying out the gestures which accompanied the words.

'What will God say to the souls of the just?'
'God will say to the souls of the just "Come ye (ranks of small arms beckon and draw into self embrace) blessed of my Father, possess ye the kingdom prepared for ye".'

'What will God say to the souls of the damned?'

'God will say to the souls of the damned, "Depart from me, ye cursed (arms fly out to the right, planned slapstick accidents occur throughout the room, the boy backhands the boy to the right, who has swiped the girl to his right, who in turn has garrotted a taller lad to her right) into everlasting flames (fingers jab toward the floor, the nearest thigh gets poked, fingers stub on desks, books in ready piles for distribution tumble to the floor) which were prepared for the devil and his angel".

Hysteria grips the scene, small faces contort with suppressed laughter; here and there, hands grip sides or genitals to suppress the pain of mirth or a sudden urge to piss. The outrage of the catechism-waiving teacher only adds to the glory of the mayhem.

'Get out, you clown!' A boy dragged from his seat by the ear.

'Silence, clowns!' the baritone depth of the hippo female in full flight accompanied by smacks round offending ears – or any ears.

In the infants' school he was imprisoned by older boys in a toilet cubicle from which he escaped by crawling 'belly-flopper under the wooden bays through pools of piss'. But there were lighter moments, as when the girls in a segregated playground captured a boy to be kissed by the girl who had ordered the kidnap, or when girls doing handstands could be observed with inverted skirts and knickers and bare waists wholly exposed. An engagement with knickers and his sexual development repeats itself throughout the book, with one account of helpful girls revealing to this reviewer that Lancashire lasses were not as forward as those from County Durham or, if they were, it was harder to find them as a Primitive Methodist.

In the primary school he was told nothing of the eleven-plus. Others were selected for practice with former 11-plus papers. When he sat the tests he provided a proper ending for the 'comprehension' story, while ignoring the questions at the bottom about the meaning of words that he did not understand. Not only did he fail, but at secondary school he was selected for the 'C' stream, which every teacher hated. It was a school that regarded his use of a public library as a matter requiring investigation. Later, he became a mineworker and, much later, he was to become a day-release university student, a political activist, and a writer whose autobiography is authentic, essential social history.

Confession provided him with a defining experience. After one of the 'more daring sorties behind the class cupboard door', he thought it best to mention it for fear of meeting his maker in an unblessed unforgiving state. He decided to slip in the real sin amongst the more regular misdemeanours.

'Bless me, Father, for I have sinned, it is three weeks since my last confession ... I have been bad tempered. I have back-answered my mother and father, I have told lies, I have been immodest, I have missed prayers, I have not had communion for three weeks since, Lord forgive me and by thy will I will never sin again.'

All the while the priest whispered, 'Yes, Yes, Yes.' Not noticed? Then, in a deep resounding Galway voice: 'Tell me now, son, and how was it you were immodest?'

'Well,' I felt myself getting hot, 'I touched another's body, Father'.

'Now, was it a girl or a boy, my child?' Me lips were getting dry.

'A girl, Father.'

'And where did you touch her body, my son?' I hadn't banked on this ... the courage all gone now.

'Her stomach, Father, her stomach.'

'Is that where you touched her?'

'Yes, Father, her stomach.' I thought of somewhere lower and thought God would think my sexual navigation was out of order again and tried to conceal the thought of that thought in case he seen that as well.

'Well, son, if this is a good confession, you must say five Hail Marys and four GlorybetotheFathers.'

A sinner, I left and went to the rail, to reason that it was a farce. Marx had said it was opium. The Little Lenin Library, from which I intended to be a little Lenin, explained the world in material ways: you were in a church of fear, now was the time to break it. I walked from the church, no longer clean. Gabriel kept his pad intact. The row at home came later.

Eight pages of dedications of a book is unusual. In this they start with 'The ancient echo of a Celtic Northumbria'. The list with many comments added includes mention of a Scottish republican army and John Lilburne, founder of the Levellers (1649), jailed by Cromwell, and eventually

> *To the hundreds of jailed, beaten, sacked and blacklisted insurgent men, women and children of the coalfields of Northumberland and Durham who fought back with everything that flesh and blood could muster in the great battle of 1984/5.*

The author explains that much of his story (through the Campaign for Nuclear Disarmament, the Young Communists, Anarchists, Trotskyites, the Young Unemployed Workers League, his time as a hippie free love advocate, and work as a trade union activist) 'sails close to the wind of illegality'. He admits to having blurred some events and changed some names because particulars may still be 'on file'. But he is at pains to state that his endnotes are often supported by contemporaneous notes and diaries, which link his story to verifiable events and the social context in which he experienced them. The Geordie dialect, which he writes with phonetics of his own devising, is clearly important to him, but, as he says, it is 'a bugger to read'. Fortunately, he doesn't do it all the time, and a limited glossary of words helps with translation.

His account of his runaway marriage to the youthful Maureen required a move from County Durham to more challenging mining employment in South Yorkshire, and signals an impetuousness to be found later. Photographs of his family and of Maureen suggest the support of loving relationships. More remains to be learned about the artistic, politicised Maureen, with hints of how liberated women might behave.

His work as a mineworker, even at a coal face designated for training, involved him in some of the most demanding tasks for a person of his delicate physique in an environment so hot that men worked naked but for boots, cap lamp battery belt, and helmet. His description of the technology is detailed, accurate and clear, and his determination to cope with such employment, without endorsing it as reasonable, is remarkable. He also had to cope with the bullying offered by a particularly hostile workmate. When he confronted the bully, and threatened to attack him at the throat with a compressed air pick, the bullying stopped. He also found that it had earned him the respect of the team. He recalled his father's words; 'The men will break your heart, son', but observed, near the end of this first volume, that 'It would take years and years to win the respect of these men but once it is achieved you can take it to the bank for it is like gold'.

Christopher Gifford

Media Lens

David Edwards and David Cromwell (Media Lens), *Newspeak in the 21ˢᵗ Century*, Pluto Press, 304 pages, hardback ISBN 9780745328942, £55, paperback ISBN 9780745328935, £16.99

> *'Princes and priests soon saw an enemy in the press. Type was in their opinion the most serious form that lead could take ... The rich classes – otherwise the conspiring classes – shut out as far as they could all knowledge of their doings, alleging that their object was to prevent the dissemination of "heresy and immorality".'*
>
> George Jacob Holyoake

Back in the mid-seventies, I was working for BBC television in Glasgow when a group called the Glasgow University Media Group (GUMG) published a book entitled *Bad News,* which covered research they had been conducting into bias in the media. It caused such a stir amongst the journalists that I worked with that it prompted me to buy a copy. The problem with the journalists was that they could not accept that the reports they turned in could in any way carry bias.

Now I have come across a book written by members of Media Lens, a group of academics and activists who encourage readers to challenge the received view of the world presented by major newspapers and broadcasters. *Newspeak in the 21ˢᵗ Century* by David Edwards and David Cromwell exposes the arrogance and servility to power of leading journalists and editors. This recalls George Orwell's proposed preface to *Animal Farm*:

> 'The sinister fact about literary censorship ... is that it is largely voluntary. Unpopular ideas can be silenced, and inconvenient facts kept dark, without the need for any official ban.'

In the thirty-five intervening years since *Bad News*, technology has changed the ways in which news is delivered, increasing the breadth of methods of delivery from TV, radio and print medium to a whole host of electronic delivery systems which multi-millionaire media moguls have tried, with some success, to monopolise.

However, the open access of the system, its interactivity, the wide spread availability of computing power, and the ability of this capacity to be used for the analysis of news corporations' output has meant that much more sophisticated methods and more robust findings can be added to the early pioneers' headline counts and measurements of column inches.

The archiving of transcripts of reports and comments on newsworthy issues has permitted the use of sophisticated search programmes which improve research accuracy and speed. The use of e-mail to beard the offending journalists on their Blackberrys has added a new level of scrutiny to the system. Further, and as this book amply illustrates, it is possible to direct readers to the authors' sources on the internet.

An issue analysed in *Newspeak* is the Israeli operation 'Cast Lead', that began in December 2008, in which they killed 1,400 Palestinians in the ghetto called the Gaza Strip. To set the context, Edwards and Cromwell refer to a Glasgow University Media Group web page (http://www.gla.ac.uk/centres/mediagroup/media/israel_excerpt2.pdf). I shall not précis it except to say that it warns us that the viewer's basic knowledge of an issue should not be taken for granted.

Of great concern to the authors is the position of the BBC during this conflict, with questions as to whether it is taking sides, or has lost its spine on tricky issues. The contribution by Tim Llewellyn, the BBC's former Middle East correspondent, voices his knowledgeable apprehensions on this count (http://www.medialens.org/alerts/04/040115_Ducking_Palestine_1.HTM).

Issue is taken with the distortion of language in one of Media Lens' archived reports, which forensically dissects the meanings ascribed to 'arrested' and 'kidnapped'. Ironically, this includes a piece by the BBC's reporter, Alan Johnstone, who would have had time to ponder the semantic niceties of this conundrum whilst he himself was held captive in Gaza (http://www.medialens.org/alerts/06/060630_kidnapped_by_israel.php).

In order to show that there is clear supporting evidence by official bodies for an alternative perspective, you can refer to a UN Refugee Agency report on the whole mess (http://www.unhcr.org/cgi-bin/texis/vtx/refworld/rwmain?docid=47baaa262).

How this was taken up by the BBC is to be found here (http://news.bbc.co.uk/1/hi/world/middle_east/7281711.stm).

Comment on operation Cast Lead from Seumas Milne provides support for a different perspective, and can be found in full (http://www.guardian.co.uk/commentisfree/2008/dec/30/israel-and-the-palestinians-middle-east).

Excerpts from BBC Middle East Editor Jeremy Bowen's diary of the conflict between Hamas and Israel are online (http://news.bbc.co.uk/1/hi/world/middle_east/7822048.stm). Bowen found himself in hot water after heavy pressure on the BBC Trust from Zionist groups, to which the Trust caved in.

And, finally, to restore faith in the human race, Noam Chomsky's article provides a necessary antidote to our pusillanimous guardians at the state broadcasters (http://www.zcommunications.org/znet/viewArticle/20316). Always remembering that lesser reporters than Bowen will have absorbed the message that the BBC's own staff cannot have confidence that the spineless BBC Trust will support them.

Media Lens has transformed the study of news media bias in that it is actively providing activists with ammunition, as foreseen by Holyoake back in the 19th Century.

Henry McCubbin

Herald Angels

George Lansbury, *The Miracle of Fleet Street: the story of the Daily Herald*, Spokesman Books, 178 pages, paperback ISBN 9780851247663, £15.00

This is not exactly the whole story of what, in the early 1930s, was to become Britain's biggest-selling daily newspaper. Those wishing to learn about the ferocious pre-Second World War circulation battles, or the anguished slide that saw the paper metamorphose into the short-lived IPC *Sun* before being given garish new clothes and soaring away under the control of fledgling emperor Rupert Murdoch, must look elsewhere.

Having been born in 1911 as a daily strike-bulletin when London print Unions came out for a 48-hour working week, and resurrected the following year with capital of around £300 as a co-operative Labour venture, the *Herald* had been publishing consistently for only 13 years when Labour leader-to-be Lansbury recounted its trials and tribulations – there were many – on the way to relative stability.

An editorial published on October 26, 1912 told of the campaign to put the paper on a sound financial footing and how a woman had visited the House of Commons to tell Lansbury: 'My husband has sent me with this message. "We have only saved a little, but here is £50. Do not let the *Daily Herald* die".' A Socialist parson presents a cheque for £150, while 'another man' said: 'Let the landlord go hang for his rent. I am sending it to you.' 'Was there ever a daily newspaper that had such wonderful support as we are getting?' asked the editorial.

Probably not. But never before or since has there been a similar David of a newspaper struggling against the Goliath of capitalism, on behalf of which most newsprint manufacturers later refused to supply a paper that was pro-women's suffrage and supported both the Russian revolution and trades union strikes. Agents scoured the country to buy paper secretly.

Having been able to publish only weekly during the First World War, the *Herald* campaigned on behalf of workers both in print and with a series of rallies, another of which was planned, to support Labour and to announce that daily publication would shortly be resumed, in November 1918 at the Royal Albert Hall. Four days before the meeting, with 19,000 people having requested tickets, the Hall management cancelled the contract, citing 'demonstrations of a revolutionary nature' at previous meetings. Time for the workers of the world to unite: the Electrical Trades Union removed all the fuses from the Hall and suggested that unless permission to use it was restored the whole of Kensington might be plunged into darkness. Oh, and no trains would stop at local stations and taxi drivers would not ply for hire near the Hall. Thousands had to be turned away from the two meetings that subsequently took place.

From its very beginning the *Herald* produced challenging journalism – the headline 'Women and children last!' swiftly followed the loss of the *Titanic*, which sank and drowned more than half the children travelling in steerage as the first issue of the paper was going to press. Observed the *Herald* of the White Star Line's profits: 'They have paid 30 per cent to their shareholders and they have sacrificed 51 per cent of the steerage children.'

Most opposition papers remained hostile to the *Herald,* and after Lansbury visited Russia in 1920, Lloyd George's Government proclaimed it had evidence that diamonds brought to London by a Russian delegation had sold for between £40,000 and £50,000 and the 'Bolshevik gold' donated to the paper. The *Herald* famously insisted that 'NOT A BOND, NOT A FRANC, NOT A ROUBLE', though confirming that £75,000 had been offered and pointing out that 'if we accepted the offer from Russia (with which this country has been technically at peace since 1855 ...), we should have done nothing dishonourable and we should not be at all ashamed of ourselves'. Such intrigue, such drama; what a movie the early years of the *Herald* would make.

Lansbury, an MP and the chief shareholder early on, became editor by accident, pitchforking himself into the role for a nine-year tenure in1913 after several predecessors had lurched from one calamity to another. 'How many more years of life remain for me, it is impossible to say,' he wrote, 'but whatever the future may be ... nothing can happen to me which will bring me more satisfaction or more joy than the memory of these great years spent in company with, and service for, the readers and friends of the *Daily Herald.*'

The paper was owned from 1922 by the TUC and the Labour Party, with Odhams Press obtaining 51 per cent in 1929. Lansbury lived to see sales top two million in1933 and died seven years later, long before his dreams were shattered by savage decline and the beginning of the end with the 1961 takeover by IPC, then a publishing giant dominated by Mirror Group. In republishing Lansbury's long-neglected book – a love story encumbered only by too much detail of political skirmishes – Spokesman has restored an important chapter of newspaper and social history.

Bill Hagerty

Reproduced from the British Journalism Review, *Volume 20 Number 4, available from SAGE Publications, 1 Oliver's Yard, 55 City Road, London EC1Y 1SP. Subscription hotline: +44 (0)20 7324 8701. Email: subscription@sagepub.co.uk*

Iraq confidential?

Ron Suskind, *The Way of the World: A story of truth and hope in the age of extremism*, Pocket Books, 448 pages, paperback ISBN 9781847391506, £8.99

This book came to my attention through Iraq Inquiry Digest*, an informative commentary on the Iraq Inquiry, which is proceeding in London under the chairmanship of Sir John Chilcot.

The Way of the World is particularly interesting because it sheds just a little light on the activities of Sir Richard Dearlove, who was head of Britain's Secret Intelligence Service from 1999 to 2004, whilst the war on Iraq was being prepared and then prosecuted. Curiously, Sir Richard has not yet appeared before the Iraq Inquiry in public session, nor has their been any suggestion that he has met with Sir John or other Committee members in private. Has he not been invited to appear? Has he refused to do so? Has the Secret Intelligence Service refused him permission to testify? We simply do not know. But there is a gaping whole in the record which the Chilcot Committee is busily compiling as long as it hasn't heard from the head of the Secret Intelligence Service. It was during his watch that Britain joined with the United States in the invasion of Iraq, and became an occupying power in that country whilst hundreds of thousands of its people died, many of them suffering violent deaths.

It is not the case that Sir Richard eschews public exposure. Ron Suskind, prize-winning journalist and author of this intriguing read, called on him in his rooms at Pembroke College in Cambridge, where he is Master. Suskind had travelled to Cambridge to ask Dearlove about what Suskind says was a last-ditch attempt by British Intelligence to avert the war on Iraq. A contact of Suskind's in Washington had informed him that, apparently, a senior SIS officer called Michael Shipster had meetings with the head of Iraqi intelligence, beginning in Jordan in early 2003.

The Iraqi apparently told Shipster that there were no weapons of mass destruction (confirming what other another well-placed Iraqi had told the UN weapons inspectors). He explained why this was the case, and how Saddam was worried that his neighbours, especially Iran, would discover that he no longer had any such deadly weapons. Suskind continues:

> 'Dearlove confirms all this. Then cuts me off. "How do *you* know about Shipster's visit?" Only very few people, he mumbles, on either side of the Atlantic, know any of this ... "Yes, it did happen",' he adds.

According to Suskind, Dearlove goes on to confirm that

> 'Shipster's precious haul of intelligence was passed immediately, by February, to Washington. Everyone "at the top" knew all about it – he and Tenet [CIA chief], Blair, Bush, and Cheney.'

Why risk such a dangerous mission at the eleventh hour? According to Dearlove, it was an 'attempt to try, as it were, I'd say, to diffuse the whole situation ...'

Dearlove apparently travelled to Washington to brief the Americans personally on what the head of Iraqi intelligence had told Shipster about Iraq's non-existent WMD. Tenet's intuition was that they wouldn't want to hear this 'downtown'. He was right, it seems. Dearlove summarised the response in his 'conversation' with Suskind in this way:

> 'The problem was the Cheney crowd was in too much of a hurry, really. Bush never resisted them quite strongly enough ... Yes, it was probably too late, I imagine for Cheney ... I'm not sure it was too late for Bush ... I don't think it was too late for Bush.'

Suskind has extraordinarily good access to the top of what is nominally Britain's Secret Intelligence Service. From Cambridge he travelled to London to meet Nigel Inkster, Dearlove's number two at MI6, assistant director until 2006. Inkster is also forthcoming in his conversation with

Suskind, just as his former boss was, although he does contradict the Master of Pembroke about whether the Shipster mission was too late to avert the war. Inkster first confirms that Tahir Jalil Habbush was Shipster's contact in Iraqi intelligence. Then he goes on to say:

> 'You have to bear in mind that at that point the UK and the US were in very different positions. I think within the USA there was widespread resignation that this was going to go ahead … and it was already more about preparing for the aftermath. Whereas within the UK, of course, the whole thing went right down to the wire. And everyone was trying to find a way out, if that could be done … You know, the feeling was that this was a decision the US had made way back and, you know, that was the defining perception.' The United States was 'like a runaway train. There was nothing that was going to stop this.'

The purpose of the Shipster mission was to 'get inside Saddam's head,' according to Inkster. Suskind interprets Inkster to mean that 'It's what Blair wanted'.

Are these not extraordinary claims? There has been no mention of Shipster's mission at the Iraq Inquiry, as far as I know. Nor can his name be found in Lord Butler's *Review of Intelligence on Weapons of Mass Destruction*, which was published in July 2004. Shouldn't this episode be scrutinised? Did it really happen? If so, what does it tell us about the frantic weeks during early 2003 as the armies were readied to invade Iraq, and the 'troublesome' Attorney-General was sent to Washington to 'put some steel in his spine'?

Sir John Chilcot said at the conclusion of Clare Short's memorable testimony that one of the two tasks of the Inquiry was 'to establish a reliable account of what happened from many people's different perspectives'. The second task was to 'identify serious lessons to be learned from the whole experience'. Shouldn't the Shipster mission be probed on both counts?

Tony Simpson

Korea

David Halberstam, *The Coldest Winter: America and the Korean War*, 736 pages, Macmillan hardback ISBN 9780230709904, £25, Pan paperback ISBN 9780330458504, £9.99

'If we just stand by, they'll move into Iran and they'll take over the whole Middle East. There's no telling what they'll do if we don't put up a fight now.'

The refrain will be familiar to students of US interventionism in the Cold War era; on this occasion, the speaker was Harry Truman, and the warning related to the North Korean crossing into the South in June 1950, an act viewed by the United States' National Security Council as a flagrant breach of the UN Charter. Perhaps rather more pertinent was the remark, attributed to the Japanese politician Rikitaro Fujisawa, that 'Korea lies like a dagger, ever pointed towards the heart of Japan'. If the North Korean leadership had hoped that the United States would regard the matter as a purely internal dispute and adopt an impassive stance, as it had done during the civil war in China, they were to be disappointed. In fact, the communist revolution in China had provided US policymakers with what they considered to be irrefutable evidence of the dangers of non-intervention. Russia had succumbed to the 'Red menace' decades earlier, but she was never believed to lie within the US sphere of influence; by contrast, as Halberstam explains, 'China was America's, and thus had been lost by America'.

The sense of a nation waking from a complacent lull is a consistent theme of this immense history of the Korean conflict. This was a conflict which shattered a number of enduring myths: the disastrous military setbacks suffered by the US in the early part of the campaign shattered the illusion that military power rested only with the richest, most technologically advanced nations, and exposed the limitations of US power barely five years after its aircraft Enola Gay and Bockscar delivered to Japan two of the 20th Century's most horrific crimes against humanity, and seduced US policymakers into dreams of global omnipotence backed by nuclear might. Also destroyed was the myth that US politics stopped at the water's edge; the intensity and bitterness of the domestic political disputes, which comprise a complex and fascinating sub-plot in Halberstam's account, heralded the end of the political bipartisanship of the World War Two period.

The US involvement in Korea acted as a midwife to the National Security Council 68 (NSC 68) project of Dean Acheson and Paul Nitze. NSC 68 offered Americans a new framework for interpreting world affairs in the post-World War Two era; it defined global conflict in unequivocally ideological terms, demanding enormous budget increases for the global struggle against the Soviet Union. President Truman had been stalling over the proposed programme when the perceived imperative of Korean intervention provided a timely kick-start; the Pentagon budget quadrupled from £13 billion to £55 billion in autumn 1951, a significant shift of gear that paved the way for four decades of ideologically-driven global interventions characterised by venal, murderous cynicism (or, if you read the newspapers, bumbling altruism).

Another common theme is the sheer incompetence of senior policymakers on both sides: 'Every key decision on both sides,' explains Halberstam, 'turned on a miscalculation': the US underestimated the skills of the North Korean troops, and overestimated how well prepared the US troops were; the US drove north of the 38th parallel despite Chinese warnings; MacArthur insisted on pushing his forces all the way to Yalu, convinced that the Chinese would not come in; Mao in turn had too much confidence in his soldiers' revolutionary spirit, and pushed his troops too far south, suffering heavy losses; Stalin also miscalculated – the Russian failure to support the Chinese in the vital early months caused deep divisions which culminated in the Sino-Soviet split; Kim Il Sung miscalculated, convinced as he was that the peasants of the South would rise up in defence of a unified Korea. The ultimate beneficiaries were those in the US State Department who were intent on manipulating the communist threat for the purposes of building and consolidating a national security state. Halberstam notes that Chinese entry into the conflict 'gave the ultimate push forward to the vision embodied in NSC 68. It greatly increased the Pentagon's influence and helped convert the country toward more of a national security state than it had previously been.'

Perhaps inevitably, there are occasional hints at the author's own political bias, such as Halberstam's rather unsatisfactory appraisal of the communists' mass appeal among rural Chinese workers ('All they had to do was exploit the country's myriad grievances and miseries'). In contrasting the 'democratic' South with the authoritarian North, Halberstam glosses over the fundamentally anti-democratic nature of the South Korean regime for much of the Cold War period. And there is the occasional stylistically and syntactically questionable form of words where the author seems to overreach himself in a bid to achieve added literary effect ('Stalin … would have ruled almost exactly like Kim Il Sung and survived … till death did him part [sic].').

This is, nonetheless, an extremely valuable book and an enjoyable read, comprehensive in its scope and thoroughly researched. In addition to meticulously analysing the domestic and international political dimensions of the conflict, Halberstam writes at length about the experiences of the soldiers who fought in it, giving *The Coldest Winter* a very welcome social dimension.

Nathaniel Mehr

China

Yasheng Huang, *Capitalism with Chinese Characteristics: Entrepreneurship and the State,* **Cambridge University Press, 366 pages, hardback ISBN 9780521898102, £15.99**

Since the late 'seventies, the Chinese economy exploded into a phenomenal new surge of growth. This book is the latest attempt, and a very serious one, to explain why this is.

Yasheng Huang is severely orthodox: he sees economic development as resulting from private ownership, with attendant property rights, deregulation and liberalisation. He devilled his acute knowledge of the empirical basis for his judgements from intense labour among the official documents, paying special attention to the relevant documents from banks. From this perusal, he identified the complete inadequacy of a gradualist approach to the Chinese reforms. Of course, economic reforms are one thing: democratic experiments completely another. Perhaps modern China is approaching another crossroads, since the economic upswing may prove unsustainable in the absence of greater democracy.

But up to now, an impoverished countryside has fed vast reservoirs of labour into the growing towns and their industries. In Tientsin the leader of the city's trade unions explained this to me in the early 'nineties: 'We in China have an unlimited supply of cheap rural labour', he said. 'But once they are acclimatised to industrial life', I asked him, 'will they not develop larger appetites?' 'Not very quickly', he said. 'There are plenty more workers from the countryside who will wish to do their jobs if they are discontented.'

Huang argues that there are two Chinas: an entrepreneurial one in the rural areas, and a predominantly State controlled urban regime. In the 1990s, he explains, urban China asserted itself over and above its rural complement.

This book begins with a detailed synopsis, which helpfully sets out the prospectus. Huang pays special attention to the development of Shanghai, which was among the least reformed of the urban economies in the 1980s, and yet its leaders during the second half of that decade went on to dominate Chinese politics through the 1990s.

The market in China has engendered fewer new private sector businesses than generally assumed. Regulation was stricter in Shanghai than elsewhere, but the share of labour income, including the income of proprietors, was very low. Teasing through the contradictory faces of

Shanghai's development, Huang leads us to confront a reality which is frequently over-simplified in the West.

Social unrest has clearly increased in the most recent years in China, and Huang gives this his attention.

'Protests in China increased at a stunning rate. Between 1993 and 1997, the total number of demonstrations rose from 8,700 to 32,000. According to official figures released by the Ministry of Public Security, there were 58,000 large-scale incidents of unrest in 2003, 74,000 in 2004, and 87,000 in 2005. In an ominous development, in September 2007, more than 2,000 demobilised soldiers rioted simultaneously in two cities 770 miles apart from each other, indicating a high level of co-ordination.'

And so this profoundly informative book about Chinese capitalism concludes with the perception that the Chinese working class is beginning an awakening. Watch this space.

Ken Coates

Cuba

Helen Yaffe, *Ché Guevara: The Economics of Revolution*, Palgrave Macmillan, 368 pages, hardback ISBN 9780230218208, £55.00, paperback ISBN 97802302182115, £17.99

This book covers a relatively short period of Ché Guevara's life, namely the six years he spent in the nascent revolutionary Cuban government from 1959 to 1965. The period might have been relatively short but he used it to great effect, providing the driving force for the transformation of the semi-colonial economy of Cuba and putting it firmly on the path of socialist transition. We are familiar with Ché the committed guerrilla fighter, determined to hasten Third World liberation, but we are perhaps not so aware of Ché the socio-economic theorist, banker, administrator, trade diplomat, technical innovator and industrial moderniser. Helen Yaffe has made a comprehensive and thorough effort to redress this gap in our knowledge. The book captures the enormous energy of Guevara, both in his practical and theoretical activity, and charts the reciprocal dynamism and interplay of practice and theory when he was head of the National Bank of Cuba and, later, Minister for Industry.

Guevara initially took charge of the National Bank of Cuba and wasted little time in securing Cuban gold and international currency reserves from the clutches of the United States. The reserves being held at Fort Knox would most certainly have been impounded as Cuban-American relations plummeted. Again, to forestall any undermining of the national currency, Guevara ordered the printing of new banknotes. In the short term these measures helped to protect the Cuban economy from both internal and external enemies. In the long term, the problems faced by the Cuban economy were daunting, and the book explains these difficulties in detail. Briefly, the major problems included dependency on a sugar-producing agricultural monoculture, structurally high unemployment and underemployment, chronic rural poverty and ill-health, foreign monopoly control of many industries and resources, mass illiteracy, and the mass exodus of many of the middle-class professionals, technicians and administrators.

The main substance of the book is how Guevara dealt with these difficulties, and the theoretical premise on which he acted to ensure that, by 1961, Cuba was placed firmly on a socialist economic path, despite the US economic blockade. Of course, Cuba needed help and the Soviet bloc, and the Soviet Union in particular, was able and willing to give vital assistance, much of which was negotiated by Guevara. Negotiating these trade agreements occasioned extended visits to the Soviet bloc and also Yugoslavia, from which he was able to obtain a firm grasp of the realities of their economies. He was not impressed, realising the relative backwardness of technology in the Soviet bloc (with the exception of the defence industry) in comparison to the United States. Neither did he regard their organisational methods to be effective in comparison with what he had gleaned from reading the internal planning documents from Western Corporations that had been expropriated in Cuba. He regarded the methodology of Western corporate organisations in planning control, accountancy and, above all, cost control to be far superior to its Eastern bloc equivalent. But for Guevara there was an even greater hazard in absorbing the Soviet organisational routines, and their use of 'competition, the profit motive, material incentives, credit, and interest (expressions of the law of value)'. Guevara was to develop his own alternative to the Soviet methodology, and the conflict between these two paradigms became known as the 'Great Debate', the ramifications of which have waxed and waned through Cuban political and economic life up to the present. The 'Great Debate' and the striving to do things differently in Cuba, instigated primarily by Ché Guevara, forms the core of this book.

The 'Great Debate' coincided with additional efforts to 'liberalise' the Soviet economy and introduce some further elements of 'market socialism', already largely operational in Yugoslavia (but there with workers' self-management). Through such changes it was hoped that the problems of economic stagnation and the continuing growth of bureaucracy could be overcome. The work of the Ukrainian academic Evsei G. Liberman gained prominence, in which it was suggested that the enterprise's drive for profit should be the gauge of productivity, not the central plan, utilising the stimulus of material incentives. There is not space to go into the intricacies of the debate, and it cannot be boiled down alone to the rivalry between moral and material incentives. The argument ranges over a number of topics: the relationship of the enterprises to each other, and their lack of control from the centre; the role of the central bank; the degree of central planning; pricing policy and the use of the law of value as propounded by Marx. Guevara became convinced that if the capitalist norms of control, those utilising the profit motive and material incentives, were applied, together with allowing relative independence for enterprises to compete, then you would see an erosion of any socialist consciousness amongst the workforce. He became convinced that what he called the 'hybrid' system adopted by the 'actual existing' socialist states would lead, eventually, to capitalist restoration, as it fostered the 'aggressive fight for profits', and detracted from the necessary 'collective consciousness' needed to foster the struggle for a socialist outcome. The debate overflowed to encompass the participation of various eminent foreign Marxists, amongst them Charles Bettelheim and Ernest Mandel, while Guevara wrote at least 20 articles on related matters in several Cuban journals and touched on the question in numerous public speeches. The debate opened up the question of 'transition economics' again, resuscitating the debates of the early years of the Bolshevik state: 'war communism', the New Economic Policy and, of course, the dogma of 'socialism in one country' all had an airing.

In outline, Guevara's policy, as laid out in his *Budgetary Finance System*, as opposed to the Soviet model of the *Auto Financing System*, is as follows:

● Workplaces of a similar industrial type were to be grouped into 'consolidated enterprises' and controlled centrally.

● These enterprises would not have funds of their own, but would use money as a unit of account to record productivity, subsequently analysed centrally.

● The National Bank would control the flow of funds to enterprises in accordance with the requirements of the National Plan.

● Moral incentives are to be of paramount importance in the long run, with material incentives necessary only in the short term.

● Every effort should be made to encourage the growth of a socialist consciousness coupled with appeals for additional voluntary labour, education of workers, and administrators should be given a high priority.

● The Law of Value will still exist but will be progressively undermined by central planning and the 'new social relations'.

● Cost control will be stressed, and increases in productivity be measured by that yardstick.

● Costs will be the criterion used to judge the success or failure of the enterprise or technique, not the pursuit of profit.

● The costs of Cuban industry will determine price, and will be compared to international prices to judge their productivity.

Yaffe's book explains much of this in detail in the context of the many factors involved, and the difficulties faced by the Cuban transitional economy, both its historical handicaps and the ever present external threats, such as the US economic blockade. The essence of Guevara's position was to persuade the Cuban workforce (and the rest of the population) to view their economic efforts through the prism of socialist consciousness, the national economy as one industry, one factory, with a collective sense of purpose.

One of the things that Yaffe's book makes clear is the incredible intellectual and physical energy of Guevara during this period, and the amazing number of activities he initiated and was involved in. In the context of 'The Great Debate' he was studying Marx's *Capital* plus many other classic Marxist texts, and other literature from east and west, which discussed market socialism. Within the Ministry of Industry he organised weekly seminars on Marx's *Capital:* starting at nine in the evening and often not finishing till the early hours, the participants included vice-ministers, advisers and invited guests. The discussions were led by Professor Anastasio Mansilla, a Soviet selected intellectual, who we can be certain got more discussion than he bargained for. Education and training were key tools in fostering moral incentives, and workers, administrators, directors of consolidated enterprises, right up to vice-ministers were encouraged to participate. Wage differentials were utilised to encourage training and a scale of eight rates, with the top rate three times the bottom rate, was employed. This concession was defended by Fidel Castro who proclaimed, 'the revolution cannot equalise incomes overnight' ... but our ... 'aspiration is to arrive at equal incomes'. The need for mass training at such a breakneck speed was in part occasioned by the skills exodus: for example, two-thirds of public accountants had left Cuba by 1961, and of the 800 who were left, virtually all were based in the Havana area. Such a situation would, of course, make difficult the cost analysis and control which was to replace the profit motive.

Together with the drive to educate and train the workforce, Guevara encouraged workers to be both inventive and innovatory. One campaign was called 'Construct Your Own Machine', and another initiated a 'Committee for Spare Parts', as a response to the increasing difficulties caused by the American blockade. Consultation, management, participation and inspection are dealt with comprehensively in one chapter, which also deals with the 'Plan of Demotion'. This was a scheme by which the top echelons of enterprises and the central senior administrators, such as vice ministers, would take, temporarily for a month, a subordinate role at least one level down from their full-time position. By this measure Guevara hoped to prevent the growth of élitism and bureaucracy, and to impart knowledge of the difficulties faced by subordinates. Production assemblies within enterprises were held on a regular basis, in order to 'audit the work of their administration'. They were chaired by elected workers. The purpose was to ensure that management was doing its job. Committees for Local Industry were brought into existence to ensure localised coordination and to solve problems at the local level. Finally, Guevara was to initiate research committees into computerisation (in Cuba, in 1961, there were two computers only), automation and cybernetics, and a whole host of practical scientific areas in some of which Cuba was later to excel.

This is an important and interesting book, one could almost say exciting, which is quite an achievement for a work on economics. An awful lot of ground is covered, much of it of relevance to what went wrong with the Soviet experience, and it is also instructive concerning the dangers facing any nation attempting to escape from the tentacles of global capitalism. There is perhaps another book that needs to be written, in the light of those first formative years, continuing the story from Guevara's laudable efforts up to the present situation in Cuba. A perhaps inadequate attempt is made at the end of the book to draw conclusions as to the long-term significance of Guevara's involvement, and its effect on Cuba's economy. There are signs that the strains of the 'special period', whilst largely overcome, have left deep scars, particularly amongst younger Cubans. Does this mean a change of direction towards the further use of market mechanisms? The future of Cuba and the move to the left throughout Latin America is one of the more hopeful signs that might yet put socialism back on the global agenda. It would be unthinkable to lose it.

John Daniels

Russia

Stephen F. Cohen, *Soviet Fates and Lost Alternatives: from Stalinism to the new Cold War*, Columbia University Press, 328 pages, hardback ISBN 9780231148962, £19.50

Stephen Cohen's book provides a fascinating study of some of the key turning-points and controversies in the evolution of the Soviet Union until the ultimate break-up in the early 1990s. The analysis continues with an examination of the subsequent relations between Russia and the United States.

The author is exceptionally well qualified to conduct such a study. He is an American scholar who spent much time in the Soviet Union, studied many original sources of information, and interviewed leading personalities. He is the Professor of Russian Studies and History at New York University and Emeritus Professor of Politics at Princeton University. His book is not a partisan tract in a cold war. He has much to say that is original.

His book, as suggested by its title, studies the alternatives that faced the Soviet leadership at various times since the death of Lenin. The author demonstrates that the choices made had a profound impact on the course of Soviet history.

The opening chapter deals with the ideas and role of Bukharin, the youngest of the top leadership around Lenin at the time of the Bolshevik revolution in 1917. He was barely 29 years old when the Bolsheviks took power. The author describes him as the most genuinely popular and, perhaps, the most interesting intellectual of the Communist Party leadership that forged the new Soviet state during the years of revolution and civil war from 1917 to 1921. He did not always agree with Lenin, who sometimes criticised his point-of-view and lack of dialectics. Nevertheless, Lenin held him in high esteem, describing him as the 'favourite of the entire Party'.

In 1921 Lenin initiated what was known as the New Economic Policy to overcome the devastation of civil war and foreign intervention. Alongside state-owned industries, banks and transport the Soviet leadership encouraged small-scale private enterprise in agriculture, distribution and sections of manufacture. After Lenin's death, differences emerged in the top leadership of the Communist Party about the New Economic Policy. Bukharin was one of its principal defenders. He also argued for a programme of socialist humanism.

Towards the end of the 1920s, Stalin initiated rapid industrialisation and agricultural collectivisation. His contention was that these changes were essential to accelerate socialist construction and to strengthen the Soviet Union against the ever-present threat of foreign intervention and hostility. The nominal argument was that collectivisation in agriculture should be conducted voluntarily. In reality there was often coercion, leading to a fall in production and hardship. Bukharin was strongly critical of the changes and continued to support the concepts of the NEP.

By 1929 Bukharin was stripped of most of his leadership positions, though he remained as editor of the newspaper, *Izvestia*, until his arrest in 1937. He was put on trial in 1938 and executed. He was the victim of a purge, initiated by Stalin, which affected hundreds of thousands – perhaps more – of Soviet citizens.

Many years later, in 1988, the Communist Party of the Soviet Union 'rehabilitated' Bukharin, and tributes were paid to his memory. The words of Bukharin in a letter to his wife on the eve of his arrest, when he knew that he would be executed, are among the most haunting in the history of the international movement. He wrote:

'You should know, comrades, that there is also my drop of blood on the banner which you will carry on your triumphant march to communism.'

Bukharin's ideas were to find favour many years later in the changes made by Gorbachev, not only in economic policy, but also in his commitment to human rights. Similarly, Bukharin may also have influenced the economic policy of the Chinese Communist Party after the death of Chairman Mao. The Chinese leadership accepted that market forces and private ownership had a place in socialist development, providing always that the ultimate control of the economy rested with public influence and ownership.

A dramatic turning-point in Soviet history was, of course, the denunciation by Khrushchev, in 1956, of Stalin's political repression. Khrushchev was not, however, without his own 'skeletons in the cupboard'. He had been associated with repressive measures and his style of leadership was erratic. The full potential of the changes that his presence might suggest were not fully realised.

In 1964, Khrushchev was dismissed by the Central Committee of the Communist Party of the Soviet Union (CPSU). Some of the leadership did not share his constant criticism of the Stalin period, and pointed to the economic progress that had been made, and the role of Stalin in the mobilisation of the Soviet Union to bring about the defeat of the German invasion in the Second World War. Others criticised Khrushchev's erratic behaviour, his failures in economic policy, and his dismissive attitude towards collective leadership.

The period of Brezhnev's leadership, following the downfall of Khrushchev, is described by Stephen Cohen as an era of 'conservatism'. The role of Stalin in the victory of the Second World War was emphasised, and many of Khrushchev's policies were criticised. Brezhnev was, however, not without his critics. The economy, it was said, was stagnating.

The next major turning point in the evolution of the Soviet Union was the emergence of Gorbachev as leader of the CPSU in the middle of the 1980s. This was no accident of succession. One of his predecessors, Andropov, was an able leader and a reformer, but he died before his full influence could be felt.

Gorbachev, on becoming General Secretary of the CPSU, changed many of the policies of the Brezhnev era. Beginning in 1987, more than one million victims of earlier purges were officially 'rehabilitated'. They included not only Bukharin but also many other Soviet leaders who had been purged and executed.

Stephen Cohen describes Gorbachev's contribution as Soviet leader in sympathetic terms. He sought to transform the authoritarian political system and to foster democratic change; he recognised that there was a role for market forces in a socialist state; he sought to change a Moscow dominated union of states into an authentic federation; and he sought to contribute towards ending the 'Cold War'. He also emphasised his commitment to 'human values'.

Another prominent member of the Soviet leadership during this period was often described in the West as a rival of Gorbachev who wanted to restore a more traditional style of Soviet leadership. Stephen Cohen describes him in more sympathetic terms. Ligachev was ten years older than Gorbachev, and his work spanned many years of the history of the Soviet Union. He was proud of his own role and of many others in earlier years in building the USSR and contributing to the defeat of fascism. Ligachev was also an admirer of the earlier leader, Andropov.

Despite his many achievements Gorbachev did not maintain his leadership in the reformed Soviet Union. He was followed by Boris Yeltsin, who was a very different individual in every way. Yeltsin had risen through the ranks of the CPSU, but his years of power marked the ultimate eclipse of Russia as any kind of socialist state.

Many of the people around Yeltsin saw their possession of political influence as a passport to the private ownership of resources and productive enterprises. Capitalism was restored on a grand scale, and the new 'oligarchs' accumulated immense wealth. Millions of Russian people suffered a fall in living standards. Some of the new 'oligarchs' of capitalism flaunted their wealth abroad through the purchase of expensive property, foreign enterprises and football clubs.

But this was not the final swing of the political pendulum. In the year 2000 a former KGB officer became the Russian President. His name was Putin. He is still with us, though now as Prime Minister. He is an able man and, though not a communist, he shares the pride of millions of Russians that the previous socialist state had achievements to its credit as well as grave injustices. Despite all the difficulties, the USSR became one of the world's two super-powers, and it played a decisive role in the defeat of fascism in the Second World War. Putin appears to maintain his popularity. Stephen Cohen is of the view that the United States could have done more, and could still do more, to improve relations with Russia.

This is a book to be read not only by specialists in history but also by the general reader. It deserves success.

J. E. Mortimer

Rodchenko

John Milner, *Design: Rodchenko*, Antique Collectors' Club, 96 pages, hardback ISBN 9781851495917, £12.50

Alexander Mikhailovich Rodchenko died in 1956, in his sixty-seventh year, three years after Stalin. He left an extraordinary body of work, which gives a striking impression of the changing ambitions of the Soviet Union as it struggled through the decades following the revolution in Russia of October 1917.

This handsome little volume focuses mainly on Rodchenko's graphic work, in the form of book jackets, posters and labelling for food and drink, all reproduced in glorious colour. These items tell their own stories. There is the cover of Mayakovsky's poem *Syphilis*, with its ghostly photographic negative of a person's head, which was published in Tiflis in 1927 in an edition of 5,000 copies. During the 1920s, Rodchenko's elegant lettering proclaimed the works of Ehrenburg, Aseev, Mayakovsky and other writers who gave their support to the revolution. But life was becoming even harder as the 1920s advanced, and Stalin established himself. In 1930, Mayakovsky committed suicide.

Rodchenko persevered, and his work during the 1930s reflects the increasing industrialisation of the Soviet Union, which built the tanks and aircraft that also figure extensively in his graphic output during the worst years of Stalin's purges. Yet, even during those dark times, there were notable flashes of creativity. In 1935, Rodchenko and his future wife, Varvara Stepanova, produced the stunning fold-out parachute illustration for the twelfth number of *USSR in Construction*. Printers must have cursed the specification, but this is one of the unforgettable images of the pre-war period.

John Milner, visiting professor at London's Courtauld Institute of Art, contributes a scholarly and informative commentary on Rodchenko's signal contribution to design. Following the recent landmark exhibition at the Tate Modern, *Rodchenko and Popova: Defining Constructivism* (see *Spokesman 105*), the creative imagination of Soviet pioneers reaches out to new generations.

Tony Simpson

Apartheid Again

Ben White, *Israeli Apartheid: A Beginner's Guide*, Pluto Press, 144 pages, hardback ISBN 9780745328881, £30, paperback ISBN 9780745328874, £9.99

Recent times have taught us two very important things about Israel-Palestine. On the political level and in the high sphere of the international community, Israel remains untouchable. The self-proclaimed Jewish State enjoys an impunity rarely seen in history.

Its aggression against the people of Gaza was one of the bloodiest and most ruthless in the long list of Israel's attacks on the Palestinians. Numerous inquiries by well respected organisations such as Amnesty International, *B'Tselem* (The Israeli Centre for Human Rights in the Occupied Territories), and Human Right Watch have demonstrated that the Israeli army deliberately targeted civilians, buildings and infrastructure. It bombed schools, mosques, a media centre, and UN infrastructure. Civilians were shot at while waving white flags, paramedics where maimed while picking up dead bodies in the street, white phosphorous was used in civilian areas, and Israeli soldiers testified that they had been given *carte blanche* for three weeks.

In spite of such clear violations of international human rights law and the Geneva Conventions, not one Western state came to the rescue of the

Palestinians. Subsequently, most European countries either abstained or voted against the implementation of the very thorough and balanced Goldstone Report on the Gaza Conflict during a vote at the UN General Assembly. To make matters worse, a new trade deal was struck on agricultural products between Israel and the European Union.

Even the normally powerful United States, under a new, so-called dovish administration, had to back down on its demand that settlement (the word 'colony' is actually more appropriate) building should be halted before any peace negotiations could resume between Israel and the Palestinian Authority.

On the other hand, public opinion inclines more and more towards the Palestinians and screams for justice. The gap between the peoples and their governments is huge, and is getting bigger every day. For most people, the Gaza massacre was a step too far. Huge demonstrations took place in most capital cities around the world. A hundred thousand people turned up in London in freezing temperatures, half a million demonstrated in Turkey, ten thousand chanted peace slogans in Tel Aviv. People demonstrated outside the BBC offices in London for its biased reporting of the massacre, MPs were swamped with letters of protest, fund-raising took place in community halls, churches and workplaces, and membership of Palestine solidarity groups went through the roof.

On the street, people started to ask themselves some very tough questions: 'Have we been lied to for so many years about such a crucial issue? Is the media working hand in hand with our government? Are we only free as long as we do what our government tells us? What is really happening in the Middle East?'

It is in this context that Ben White's book, *Israeli Apartheid,* came out. The sub-title of the book, *'A Beginner's Guide'*, is somehow too modest a description. This book works on very different levels and can touch a very wide range of people, knowledgeable or not about the Israel-Palestine conflict.

To start with, Ben White gives a very brief and understandable history of the conflict from the birth of the Zionist movement. After a few pages it becomes clear that this conflict and its making are in fact not that complicated and pretty easy to understand. The myth that 'this conflict has been going on for thousands of years and is too complicated to understand or be solved' quickly falls apart.

Ben White could not have done it better. To explain the present, and to make sure people not familiar with the subject grab the whole story, it was crucial to give a to-the-point and brief historical analysis.

The author then moves quickly through the years and, chapter by chapter, covers all the major topics related to Israel-Palestine: Israel as a colonialist project; the Nakba of 1948 when hundreds of thousands of Palestinians were driven from their homes; the refugee problem; the war of 1967 and the second Palestinian forced exile; the occupation of Palestinian territories; the building of the wall; the Palestinian minority inside Israel and, finally, the solidarity movement and what can be done to bring justice to the Palestinians.

By examining those topics and writing about them in a very simple, non-academic vocabulary, Ben White succeeds in making this book accessible to all audiences. In 144 pages, the author breaks down myth after myth. The Israelis claim that, in 1948, the Palestinians fled because the Arab armies ordered them to do so. How, then, can they explain that 50 per cent of the 700,000 Palestinians who fled had already gone by May 1948, when the war started? The Israelis claim that the disproportionate violence used during the second intifada was in response to Palestinian attacks. How, then, can they explain that, if the first Palestinian attack did not occur before November 2000, they had, in October, already deployed helicopter gunships, tanks, high velocity bullets and missiles?

The last part of *Israeli Apartheid* is dedicated to activism, and what we can do as citizens. This is very well done and, with the help of a thorough series of questions and answers, the author makes things easy for anyone who would like to get involved in the United Kingdom or on the ground in Israel-Palestine, complete with addresses and websites of organisations working for a just peace.

Israeli Apartheid is a vital tool for anyone who wants to understand the Palestine question better, to get involved in the struggle for *Adalah* ('justice' in Arabic), or simply to brush up their knowledge of the situation. A very useful book indeed.

Frank Barat

Yugoslavia's Destruction

Diana Johnstone, *Fools' Crusade: Yugoslavia, Nato and Western Delusions*, Pluto Press, 2002, 320 pages, paperback ISBN 9780745319506, £15.99

The Nato attack on Serbia in March 1999 could, *mutatis mutandis*, be as fateful for the 21st century as the Austrian attack on Serbia in August 1914 was for the 20th. It marked Nato's change from a defensive to an aggressive organisation, as advocated by US strategists in the early 1990s. It provided precedents for aggressive war; population expulsions under a Nato protectorate (together with the US/Nato-supported Krajina genocide); 'coercive bombing' of civilian facilities; and a mendacious propaganda campaign, including the use of a forged document, of a type previously seen only in totalitarian states. These precedents were soon followed in Afghanistan, Iraq and Lebanon.

Several of the war's architects hold important posts in the Obama Administration. In Britain, the main political parties and the press unquestioningly embraced the Blairite ethic that the United States and its allies had a right and a duty to ignore international law and the dismal history of 'humanitarian' war, and invade (unfriendly) states where 'human rights abuses' were occurring, to impose democracy and modernisation. Nato policies were not defended by rational arguments on their likely consequences (there were warnings that they would lead to genocide and a 'gangster state') but by denouncing critics as 'appeasers'. There have been no second thoughts. In contrast to many critical books on Iraq, very few on Kosovo have been published – and they have effectively been censored by not being reviewed.

All this justifies a review of Johnstone's book, even though it was published in 2002, and is not in a second edition with a Postscript (*cf.* the Postscript in www.caseagainstnato.co.uk). Johnstone's aim is to put the war in perspective and examine aspects which have been distorted or neglected – specifically the responsibility for the war; the various nationalisms in Yugoslavia; Nato's support for Albanian nationalism; the 'victors' justice' of war crimes prosecutions; and the role of Germany.

Johnstone begins by pointing out a remarkable divergence between myth and reality. The myth is that the United States has upheld peace, freedom and democracy. The reality is a long history of military interventions with disastrous consequences for the countries involved. In the century before 1939, the USA continually intervened in Latin America, imposing harsh colonial rule or – more usually – supporting friendly dictators. During the Cold War, as well as Vietnam, there were dozens of 'covert operations' in Latin America, Africa and South-East Asia, often with British support, which brought to power or supported mass-murderous dictators, or fomented civil wars. The collapse of the Soviet Union saw the extension of military intervention to Eastern Europe and the Middle East.

Johnstone brings out the complex mixture of *realpolitik*, hypocrisy and misconceptions underlying US policy on Yugoslavia. Even during the

Bosnian war, some Democratic analysts supported the dismantling of Yugoslavia, and the creation of a Moslem-dominated Bosnia, as the first step in establishing US leadership of an arc of Moslem states stretching from the Balkans through Turkey to the Gulf, a new Ottoman Empire. This interpretation makes subsequent US policy in Kosovo, Afghanistan and Iraq consistent and rational, on its terms, rather than the product of ignorance and the tendency to reduce complex problems to 'good guys versus bad guys'. However, it is hard to believe that people such as Madeleine Albright were quite so Machiavellian. In Western Europe, most journalists simply canonised the Bosnian Moslems, ethnic Albanians, and Croats, and blamed the Serbs for everything. Any mention of the massacres of Serbs in World War Two, Izetbegovic's Islamic fundamentalism and denunciation of multinationalism, or anything that questioned sole Serb responsibility for the conflict, was taboo.

Johnstone's general argument – for which she makes a good case – is that the US/Nato objective in Yugoslavia was not to ensure peace or freedom but to extend American (and, in a small way, German) influence. She does not mention Camp Bondsteel, the largest US airbase outside the United States, the construction of which was begun as soon as US troops entered Kosovo, and which could only have been achieved by secession and war. She points out that a genuinely multinational state has been replaced by hostile, fascistic/nationalistic mini-states, and sometimes suggests that Yugoslavia could have been held together. The savagery displayed by all parties makes this doubtful, but a break-up could certainly have been organised in a less destructive way. In Kosovo, the problem (like that of Ireland in 1920) was a 'dual minority' problem, and a solution needed to take account of the interests of the Kosovan Serbs, Serbia and Macedonia, as well as those of the ethnic Albanians. Johnstone shows, with chapter and verse, that US/Nato policy was simply to back the KLA and provide pretexts for war.

The book is a series of essays rather than a chronological account. There are discussions of the history of Croatia, Bosnia and Kosovo, for which some background knowledge is desirable, and a chilling account of the historical basis of German determination to destroy Yugoslavia (a First World War song 'Serbia must die' was revived). Johnstone does not mention an indispensable book by a German 'insider', General Loquai's *Der Kosovo-Konflikt; Wege in einmem vermiedbaren Krieg* (The Kosovo conflict; the path to an avoidable war). There is an examination of one-sided Western reporting, and the successful PR campaigns by the breakaway nations, including some striking examples of deliberate fabrications and some less conclusive general discussion. Johnstone's valid argument that all parties committed atrocities, and that those by Croats and Moslems were often ignored, is weakened by her glossing over of atrocities demonstrably committed by the Bosnian Serbs.

Nuggets of incisive factual evidence are interspersed with discursive and sometimes repetitive passages, so that the book is not always an easy read. Nevertheless, it is a seminal work on the Yugoslav tragedy. The bellicose columnists of the liberal British press should be forced to read it.

Graham Hallett

Civilisation

Stephen Chan, *The End of Certainty: Towards a New Internationalism*, Zed Books, 320 pages, hardback ISBN 9781848134034, £17.99

Some years ago, I had the opportunity to analyse Samuel Huntington's *Clash of Civilisations* as part of a Master's degree. Because of this I was drawn to the cover of Professor Stephen Chan's book: 'Forget … Samuel Huntington', it shouts at you, from a pure red background. Whilst reading this book, I did.

Stephen Chan doesn't just assess what Huntington meant in his lecture of 1992. (Later, in 1996, it was expanded into a book, in response to Fukuyama's *The End of History*). He gently asks deeper questions such as what is a Civilisation, and how can we live together with other Civilizations so different from our own?

Chan's philosophy in *The End of Certainty* takes a step back from Huntington's 'clash', in order to investigate the complex history of civilisation. This enables him to present his New Internationalism.

In his *Preface,* Chan tells us he was advised 'not to write this book', but I, together with most other reviewers, am very pleased he did. The complex set of philosophical essays from chapter to chapter takes the reader on a journey across continents and cultures, through centuries of history and mythology, to the Gods and back. We are educated in Zoroastrianism, Buddhism, Christianity, Islam, the Mahabharata, The Book of Job, Alexander the Great, King Solomon, the Illiad, the myth of Oedipus, African novels, Eritrea, and the videogame Assassin's Creed. The list could go on. However, Chan's book isn't so much a history of the world, as a carefully considered examination of different cultures and past civilizations and their relation to us today. As Chan argues, the 'fusing [of] different strands of Western, Eastern, religious and philosophical thought is far more likely to help us understand and move forward amidst uncertainty.'

The New Internationalism propounded in the title requires both Eastern and Western civilizations to morph slightly to accommodate one another. In Chapter 9, *Transcendence and Power*, Chan introduces the Swiss academic and Islamic scholar Tariq Ramadan. The latter 'refers to Islam as a "European religion", [and] calls equally for a "European Islam"' (p. 241). Chan, through his reference to Ramadan, seems to be suggesting that if Huntington's 'clashing' cultures allow themselves to learn a little about each other then, perhaps, the different ideas in each could drive both cultures forward together.

Chan ends his book with an example of his proposed alteration in civilization – Alexander the Great. The ancient King of Macedon created one of the largest empires in history by immersing himself in the 'learning that surrounded him in the lands he conquered' (p. 305). For Chan he was given the title 'Great because he went forth to conquer – then gave himself up to be conquered by new ideas and cultures, finally achieving a location within them where he helped them form the debates that took those cultures forward' (p. 305).

This is an ambitious work, and a fabulous and challenging read. I sincerely recommend it to all.

Abi Rhodes

Drawn

Ken Gill, *Hung, Drawn and Quartered: The caricatures of Ken Gill*, edited by John Green and Michal Boñcza, Artery Publications, paperback ISBN 9780955822827, £12

This collection of caricatures apparently owes its title to a remark made by Rodney Bickerstaff at Ken Gill's 80th birthday celebration at Congress House: 'we all know Ken was good at drawing and there were a number of trade union leaders who would have loved to see Ken drawn too, but only after he'd been hung and quartered!' We reproduce two of our favourites from this handsome collection of more than 50 drawings, which comes complete with commentaries.

TS

Ron Todd by Ken Gill

GMB@WORK

GMB

GMB@WORK

GROWTH, ACCOUNTABILITY AND DEMOCRACY IN GMB

Total GMB membership has grown by 15% in real terms over the previous five years following the adoption of the GMB@Work national organising strategy in 2005.

GMB emerged from a deep financial crisis and the threat of merger in 2004/5 with a new leadership but fewer officers and resources than at any other time. Yet by spending less and asking more of GMB Workplace Organisers GMB has turned around decades of membership and financial decline.

GMB developed a single set of 38 policies and organising approaches simply based on a common understanding of what works and what doesn't. These have been adopted and implemented in all GMB Regions and GMB Sections. But the GMB@Work strategy has five fundamental organising principles which we promote to all GMB Officials and GMB Workplace Organisers.

GMB's growth rate and the GMB@Work strategy have begun to fundamentally change the union. Four out of five members are now service workers, almost half are women, officials no longer sit on the CEC, sections have been reduced from eight to three and we have returned to an annual GMB Congress—all to focus on the core truth: that a growing GMB delivers for GMB members while a shrinking GMB lets members down.

GMB@WORK STRATEGY

1. The workplace is the building block of GMB. It is at work, rather than in the community or in the media, that working people are most able to build the collective solidarity they need to tackle the injustice and inequality they face head on.

2. Each GMB workplace is organised as if a ballot for industrial action was due. GMB need GMB members to be match fit and ready, but we also need our organisation in each workplace to be democratic, transparent and accountable every day.

3. The employers have different interests than GMB members. It is GMB members' employers who are the cause of most of GMB members' problems at work and the Union's job is to stand up for and promote members' interests, not to bury them in partnership agreements.

4. It is the process of industrial relations that builds a union. People don't join unions out of gratitude for what was done in the past but out of fear and anger for the present and hope for the future.

5. People are strongest when they organise themselves. GMB members are encouraged to find their own solutions to the problems they face. GMB members in each workplace must have the power and authority they need to make decisions and officers must stop doing for members what they can do for themselves. Workplace democracy and organising must co-exist.

JOIN GMB ONLINE AT WWW.GMB.ORG.UK